MONOLOGUES FOR EVERY AUDITION

Monologues For Every Audition

By Glenn Alterman

Smith and Kraus Publishers   2013

ISBN 9781575258638
Library of Congress Control Number: 2013947155

Typesetting and layout by: Elizabeth E. Monteleone
Cover by: Borderlands Press
Front and Back cover photo by: Robert Kim

A Smith and Kraus book
177 Lyme Road, Hanover, NH 03755
editorial 603.643.6431 To Order 1.877.668.8680
www.smithandkraus.com

The author wishes to thank the following for their help in the development of the monologues for this book. Many of these monologues were developed in the Monday Night Writers Group of The Workshop Theater Company in New York.

The Workshop Theater Company.

Scott C. Sickles (Artistic Director), Jeff Paul (Managing Director), Kathleen Brant (Producing Director), Katie Braden and Anne Fizzard (Artistic Associates)

The following actors in the Workshop Theater Company are appreciated for their help in developing many of these monologues.

Margo Hammond, Ethan Cadoff, Stephen Girasuolo, Michael Selkirk, Katie Braden, Anne Fizzard, Charles E. Gerber, Ken Glickfeld, Heather Massie, Jeff Paul, Jane Lincoln Taylor, Susan Wallack, Jed Dickson, Anna Emily Wood, CK Allen, Mick Blyer, Charlotte Hampden, Laurie Schroeder, Dee Dee Friedman, Lori Faiela, Michael Gnat, Walter Brandes, Christine Verleny, Thomas Pennacchini, Kathleen Brant, and Emily Zacharias.

Also thanks to:

Members of The Actor's Studio Playwrights and Directors Unit
The Miramax Films Writers Group
The folks over at Sony
Dr. Charles Merrill, Fran Tory,

And of course thanks to Marisa Smith and Eric Kraus, my guardian angels from Smith and Kraus, who gave me my first break with my first book of original monologues many years ago; "Street Talk—Original Character Monologues For Actors." Thanks guys.

TABLE OF CONTENTS

This is my twenty-fifth book, my tenth book of monologues. I've written over five hundred monologues in all these books. Over the years I've received hundreds of letters and e-mails from actors thanking me, commenting on the monologues, and letting me know what they'd like more (or less of) when it came to monologues they'd chose for auditions. With each new monologue and in each book, I tried to incorporate those things that read that I felt were of value.

Being an actor myself for many years, I think by now I have a really good handle on what works and doesn't work when it comes to monologues for auditions. I believe that this new book of monologues represents the best of the best. I believe I've honed the craft of writing monologues and selecting monologues from plays that are actor friendly audition winners.

Every monologue in this book, no matter what the length, has a beginning, middle and end, a story to tell, shows some emotional range, and has some entertainment value for the casting director or agent watching it being performed. Many of these characters in these monologues are multi-layered, have engaging stories to tell, and (hopefully) will be fun to work on and rehearse. The bottom line is, if you enjoy the material you're working on, if you have a "I can't wait for them to see this!" feeling about the material, you'll shine and stand out among the many actors who audition with monologues. Enthusiasm is contagious. If you're excited about performing the monologue, the casting director, agent, and director will pick up on that.

I enjoyed writing the monologues in this book immensely. And I selected only those monologues from my published plays that I felt could stand on their own and pack a wallop at an audition. But before they were chosen to be in the book they went through several screenings by playwright/ actor groups that I belong too, as well as being read by theater professionals whose opinions I trust.

I wish you the best in finding just that right monologue in this book. And I wish you all the best in your monologue auditions; go get 'em!

Good luck,

Glenn Alterman

WHY THIS MONOLOGUE BOOK IS DIFFERENT THAN ANY OTHER PUBLISHED MONOLOGUE BOOK FOR ACTORS

This is my tenth book of monologues. I wanted to do something different with this book that hasn't been in any previous monologue books. I've taken into account the comments and suggestions actors have made to me over the years. I've included features in this book that are not included in any other published monologue book. My hope is that actors looking for that "just right" monologue for their particular audition will be able to navigate through all the choices offered quickly and efficiently.

1   This book offers both monologues from *award-winning, published plays as well as original monologues* written specifically for the different types of audition actors come across.

2   The monologues are *rated according to the content of material in the monologues.* An "R" rating at the top of the monologue page immediately lets you know that that monologue contains adult material and is not appropriate for younger actors. It also lets you know that that particular monologue is not a good choice for a family friendly play or church theater audition. For those kind of auditions you might look for a monologue that has a "G" rating. Hopefully the ratings will help you pick the best material that fits into your personal aesthetic. You always want to audition with the most "appropriate" material for whatever audition you're asked to do.

3   *Each monologue has an exact running time.*

When you are informed that the monologue should be two minutes and under, you want to make sure that the monologue does fall into that time frame. There are some auditions these days that have a monitor with a stop watch who will stop you at the required time whether you've finished the monologue or not. (When you're required to have a "short monologue" prepared for an audition, you generally don't want it to run more than two or three minutes.)

4   *A large selection of one-minute monologues for those one-minute monologue auditions*

In the last few years there have been an increase in those one-minute monologue auditions. I have purposely written a large variety of one-minute monologues for actors to choose from.

5   *The first chapter of this book tells you just about everything you'll need to know to prepare for any monologue audition.*

I've interviewed many casting directors and agents in my previous books and asked them specifically what they look for at monologue auditions. That, combined with my years as a monologue/audition coach, my previous writing on the subject, sitting in at many auditions, and teaching classes on monologues all over the world, have given me a pretty good idea of what works and what doesn't work. This first section on monologue preparations covers just about everything you'll need to know.

6   *This book suggests the best venues for each monologue.*
The listings let you know if it's for a theater audition, an agents office, or for an on camera film audition. Look for the *best venue suggestion* at the top of the page (before the monologue itself). Once again, these are just *suggestions.* If you feel that a specific monologue will work in another audition venue that's not listed, feel free to try it out. But always be aware of the time constraints of any audition.

Part One

Many actors underestimate the importance of having current and strong monologues that can show off their talent. An audition monologue is a marketing tool. Its sole purpose is to help you win an audition, get an agent, or showcase your acting skills to theater companies, directors and producers. Just as you should always have an up to date picture and resume, you should have at least three or four (or more) well-rehearsed, ready to go monologues. Your monologue arsenal should be replenished regularly. Often I meet actors who have been using the same monologue(s) for a year (or more). They don't understand why they get little or no response, when they've doing the same monologue(s) at countless auditions. They may be performing the monologue on "auto-pilot", desperately trying to manufacture emotions when the material no longer resonates in any way for them. It's only a two or one minute monologue and doesn't have a very long shelf life when you've been using it for a long time.

If you've found a monologue that excites you, performing it will be far more enjoyable. Passion and enthusiasm are contagious at auditions. I always tell my students you should enter every monologue audition feeling like "I can't wait for you to see me perform this! I love it and hope you will too!" If you love doing your monologue, the odds are that those you're auditioning for will enjoy it too.

How Many Monologues Do You Need in Your Monologue Arsenal?

Personally I feel you should have many monologues of different lengths, styles and emotions. At the very least, you should have two comedic, two dramatic, and one or two classical pieces. They should be well rehearsed and ready to go at a moments notice. I also feel you should have a surreal and/or a poetic piece for plays that require that type of material.

Part of auditioning for specific plays, say a Theresa Rebeck or Neil LaBut's play is being sure that the material you've selected to audition with is similar in tone to that of the play. Doing a Neil Simon comedy monologue for a David Mamet drama is an inappropriate choice.

Once you feel that any monologue you're doing doesn't "connect" for you anymore, it's time to get new material. There's certainly no shortage of monologues. I personally have nearly 6000 monologues in my monologue files. It's good to constantly update your audition material.

The Absurdity Of Doing Monologues For Auditions

I always start off all my monologue audition lectures and workshops announcing how ridiculous doing a monologue for an audition is. Look at the reality of it. I mean here you are performing a piece of material from a play (that was never meant to be used this way) to an "imaginary character", in front of a total stranger. The whole idea is kind of bizarre. That being said, it's the way of the world, at least the acting world. And there are ways to make it work.

Rehearsing a Monologue Alone Can Drive You Mad—I Know!

The biggest complaint I hear from actors I coach is how insane it is rehearsing a monologue for an audition. It's like acting in a bubble. I totally understand- and empathize. I mean there you are in your room, trying to act, say these words from a play, to an imaginary person, *and* since you're doing this alone, you also have to *direct yourself at the same time!* There is always that voice in your head, judging, saying things like "Softer" or "More Angry" or "More hurt", or, even worse" "This really stinks." "No one is going to believe this." And then, quite often there are a stream of self judgments and evaluations going on non stop, just as you're trying to act. I realize that this can make anyone crazy. The mind can only do one thing at a time. And the main thing here is for you to "rehearse and later perform the monologue."

Why Do You Need To Audition With Monologues in the First Place?

The reason that casting directors, agents, and theater companies request a monologue audition is to give them some idea of your talent as an actor. Having a reel of your professional film and TV work is certainly helpful, but sometimes agents and casting directors just don't have the time to view them. Also, many actors create reels that really don't serve them very well. The material on the reel can look amateur, be poorly lit, inaudible, feature the other actors in the scene too prominently, be too long,—and on and on. A monologue audition is immediate, live and more personal.

Monologue auditions are used to cast plays, for theater company auditions, for auditions for college theater departments, and now required more often for movie auditions, especially for independent films, or in the instance where the producers are being secretive about their screenplay.

At it's best, the monologue audition is an appetizer of your talent. It's a two-minute presentation of your talent, taste and your skill.

Selecting a monologue is a pro-active challenge. This is one of the few times in an audition situation where you are in charge. You're not waiting for anyone to "give" you anything. You have control of what you want to perform and decide how you want to perform it.

Marketing: Selecting The Right Monologue For You

What is unique about you both as an actor and as a person? I think one of the main reasons actors select inappropriate audition monologues is because they haven't really looked at what they're trying *to say* with the material they've selected. You are not only being evaluated on your talent but also on your aesthetic, your taste. One thing auditors are looking for at auditions is how appropriate the material that you've selected for yourself is. Your choice of material says so much about you. It gives them a sense of who you believe you are, both as a person and as an actor. So many actors are just too cavalier about their monologue choices. If you're an actress in your early twenties, fair and delicate looking, with a soft voice and gentle personality, then choosing a monologue that shows a hardened woman with a foul mouth and a vile temper will be inappropriate.

Actors constantly select monologues for the wrong reasons. They like the way the character speaks, the style of the writing, the subject matter, the play that the monologues comes from, etc. While these things are important, they don't answer the most important question—*Does this monologue sell who I am as an actor*? By performing it at auditions, *will they get some sense of my talent and who I am*?

The way that you work on your audition monologue is quite important. It can determine not only how effective your audition will be, but sometimes how long you'll be able to use the monologue before becomes stale.

The Mistake of Memorizing First

One of the most common mistakes actors make when starting out their work on audition monologues is to *memorize too soon*. They find a monologue that they like and instantly sit down to memorize it. Why? Once you memorize your monologue, to some degree, your final performance is "set." Even though you haven't sufficiently explored the meaning of the material, or even what the character is really trying to say, you've pre-set the results. By early memorizing you cut out one of the most important (and enjoyable) parts of the rehearsal process, *discovery*. I know that many actors prefer to memorize first, "to get the words out of the way" The question I often ask my students is, *"When you begin work on new play, would you go to the first rehearsal on the first day totally memorized?"* Generally not. Then why approach monologue material that way? A monologue is, after all, a piece of theater.

The brain memorizes in sections, patterns. When you memorize right at the start, some of how you'll be saying the words in performance is pre-set. If you'll recall, when we were children we were taught the Pledge of Allegiance. We memorized it *by rote,* the same way actors memorize their monologues. If you notice, we all say the pledge of allegiance exactly the same way. "I pledge allegiance . . . to the flag . . . of the United States of America (etc.)." Well in some ways that's how monologues sound when memorized too soon, set, fixed. You can sometimes actually hear how an actor has memorized their material by the fixed way that they perform it if they memorize too soon. There will be a certain unnatural quality to their read. I suppose that actors think that by working this way, that first they'll memorize the words, then somehow you *add on the emotions*, then layer on *blocking*, etc. It sounds like you're layering a cake, not rehearsing a monologue. Memorizing first is not an organic way to develop a role.

What I suggest is that you rehearse your monologue just like you would prepare any for any other role in a play, in a step-by-step process of rehearsing and discovery. The memorizing of the text is the last step. You'll notice that after rehearsing the monologue for a while, when you actually sit down to memorize, it'll be relatively quick and effortless. This is because you've probably retained a lot of the words during your rehearsal process.

Working From The Text

Eventually all acting begins with the text, the dialogue, the words in the play. As actors we have just one main responsibility—to be honest and truthful in our work; to make the writers character our own.

You must bring yourself and imagination to the character. You want to personalize, make it your own. I can always read the monologue myself, I don't need you to do that for me. Many actors give a "dramatic reading" of material. They give colorful line readings with generalized emotions, etc.

They're not fully engaged, there's always a distance between themselves and their work. What can you bring to the table from your life experiences and your imagination? The more you can bring of yourself to your acting, the more specific your work will be.

The First Read

The best way to start your work on a new monologue is to *simply say the words*. Don't try to perform or dramatize them. Don't recite them, just say the words *as you*. Say them the way you generally talk. Notice any initial impulses, any feelings the material brings up in you. Any impulse that you have is valid, go with it. If you have an urge to get up and move, do it. Don't question your initial responses. This is a like a first date. Everything is fresh, new, possible. Try to comprehend what you're saying as you say it. *Stay in the moment.*

If questions come up about why you feel the character is saying a specific line, you might make a note to look at that at some point?

Why does he use that particular word to express his feeling about something? Notice his thinking pattern, his actions, how he strings thoughts together in a particular sequence. What does he really mean?

After The Initial Read Through

After the initial read-through, put the monologue down, and see what stays with you. See what ideas, feelings, impressions you have. Occasionally I'll ask students questions about the material they've just read for the first time. I'm always amazed at how much insight they've gained into the character from just that first read. Those initial feelings are the launching pad for your work on the monologue.

Working Improvisationally

Many actors like to do an improvisation after their first run-through. I think working improvisationally can be very helpful in working on monologues. Put the monologue in your own words, try to express what you've learned from the text.

Select a person from your real life and use them as the imaginary other person to whom your speaking.

Subsequent Read-Through's

I like to think of the initial work on a monologue as being analogous to dipping a white sheet in yellow dye. At the beginning, the sheet is pure white. After your initial read-through (the initial dipping of the sheet) you have some first impressions (some dye has attached itself to the sheet). After that initial read, remnants of the character remains with you. After each subsequent read, just like the dipping of the sheet (and retaining more dye), you discover more and more about the character.

When rehearsing your monologue this way, try not to just mechanically say the words over and over, but continually look into the character, his world, his thoughts, his feelings. A certain phrase might become the portal into who this character is. Even a single word of dialogue may give you the handle you're looking for.

Blend your own words with the playwrights. If you continue this process of improvisations followed by reading of the text, you'll discover that certain words, phrases from the text, have stuck with you. You'll start to *retain* sections of the monologue without actually sitting down and *memorizing*. You'll also notice that the text becomes *more your own*.

Writing The Characters Biography

Another way to explore a character in a monologue that you're working on, is to write a biography about him. Based on what you've learned from the text, use your imagination to create an entire life for your character. Start out by imagining where he was born, his childhood, what his life was like growing up, his likes and dislikes, everything that you need to know to make him real for you.

Some biographical questions that you might want to cover include:

1. What's the characters name?
2. How old is he?
3. Where does he live? What is his place like? Describe it.
4. What are his likes and dislikes?
5. What are his politics?
6. What was his childhood like? Describe his family life and upbringing.
7. Is he social, a loner?
8. What is his philosophy of life? Is he an optimist or pessimist?
9. Is he single? Married? Does he have children, and if so how does he relate to them?
10. How do other characters speak about him?
11. How is this character important to the play?
12. What is the first impression someone would get when first seeing him?
13. How does he speak? Slow or fast? Does he speak with a dialect? Does he have a speech impediment of any kind (stutters, etc.).
14. How does he see the world?
15. What kind of clothes does he wear?
16. How is his self esteem? If he a confident person?
17. How does where he is right now affect him?
18. What is he like at home when so one else is around?
19. Why is he saying what he's saying, what's his motivation?
20. What does he want, what's his objective?
21. What obstacles are getting in his way, preventing him from getting what he wants?

Technical Work (Script and Acting Work)

You'll want to break down the dialogue into manageable parts. Ask yourself the following basic acting questions:

Who am I?
Where am I?
Why am I there?
What is it that I'm doing?
Why am I doing it?

The answers to these questions are generally implied in the dialogue (or given in the stage directions).

Objectives and Obstacles

Find the characters *objectives* in the monologue. What does your character want to achieve as a result of their actions?: Ask yourself, *"What do I want?"* and *"Why do I want it?"*

In a play (and monologue) the obstacles are what keep your character from accomplishing his objectives. Quite often they cause conflict between characters. See if this is apparent in your monologue. Once you discover what your character wants, then ask yourself *"What obstacles must I overcome to get what I desire?"*

Finding the Beats

What your character does to accomplish each minor objective is called a beat. The beat is a unit of action and each beat is a necessary step toward the major objective. You should always break down your monologue into beats. You should be able to state the objective and obstacle for each beat. Always ask yourself *"What am I doing?"* and *"What must be done?"*

Personalizing and Identifying

You must always make all of your acting choices personal. The more you can personally invest yourself into the character you're working on, the more effective your audition monologues (and all your acting work) will be. At auditions, auditors see so many monologues that have a "generic" feel to them. The actor hasn't personalized the monologue, made it their own.

Grounding Yourself In Your Own Personalized Given Circumstances

Another way to personalize a monologue is to add your own given circumstances to the text. This is especially effective while working on original monologues. The following are a list of questions that will help you in developing your own personalized set of given circumstances. Some of these questions might seem similar to previous ones I've discussed, but you'll notice that the focus is different here.

Where are you?

Select a real place from your real life. The more familiar the place is to you, the better. Don't be satisfied with an answer like "the house I once used to live in." Be specific, what room in that house? Specifically where are you standing in that room? Remember what the room looked like; where the clock was, the paintings, etc . . .

What time of year is it?

We behave differently on a cold winter day than on a hot and muggy summer night. Be specific as to the time of year, pick a month. Is it a cold day in February or a hot day in July?

What time of day?

Is it three in the morning or three in the afternoon? There are differences in how we respond to things at different times of the day.

What happened the moment before?

What happened right before you began speaking (doing the monologue)? The motivation for the words that you're using in the monologue quite often come as a response to what the other character just said or what just happened in the scene? Once you discover that, personalize the moment before, make it real for you. Find a scenario from your real life that's similar to that moment. You might find it helpful to even write out what the other character just said to you. If you've never had anything like that happen to you, then use your imagination. Use the magic "if".

Who are you talking to?

Choose someone from your real life that is similar to the relationship that your character has with the person that they're talking to. Look at the *essence* of that relationship. If the monologue is about a private in the army talking to a general, try to imagine what that relationship might feel like. At some point we've all been subservient to a superior. Perhaps when you were a student and you went to the principle. There might be time as a child when you had a meeting with your priest or rabbi. The more specific and truthful you can be in personalizing who you're speaking to in your monologue, the more effective it will be. *Who the other person is, and your ability to believably communicate with them is one of the keys to giving a successful monologue audition.*

Communication With The Other Character

In life when we are communicating with another person, it's like there are imaginary arrows that carry our words and thoughts from ourselves to that other person. These imaginary arrows communicate information, our intentions to that person. When these arrows hit the communication has (hopefully) been received, and what we were trying to say has been understood by the other person. At this part in the communication, the other person responds in some way. It may be a verbal response, they might say something, or it might just be a look in their eyes that lets us know "they got it." After we notice that they "got it", we continue with the conversation, going on to our next idea. How the other person responded, that look in their eyes when they got it, will flavor what you'll say next and quite often how you'll say it. This is how basic communications works. Generally, this whole process occurs quite quickly so we don't even notice or think about it. When we're communicating the arrows go from us to them and back around to us and back to them, etc. There is like a *circle of communication* that's ongoing between you and your listener. This is an important concept to understand when doing a monologue for an audition.

Your job when performing a monologue for an audition is to make the auditors believe that you are truly communicating to another person.

Most actors when rehearsing their monologue (and at the actual audition) generally pay little attention to the imaginary person that they're talking to. Perhaps they pick a spot on the back wall and talk to it. They've never really investigated what it would be like to actually say those words to a real person (from their real lives). Adding that imaginary person, then attempting to communicate with them, imagining their response as we speak, then continuing until we're through speaking, is what's required.

The more you *need* to communicate to that imaginary person, the more effective and dynamic your monologue will be. Unless you give the impression that you're actually speaking to another person, there will always be a slight flatness in your performance, no matter how good an actor you are.

Most monologues are in reality, "duologues," the other person just happens not to be saying anything at the time.

Always try to place the imaginary character that you're speaking to out front. I've seen actors place the imaginary other person right next to them, say in a car scene, thereby giving us their profile for the entire audition, not a good idea. We want to see your eyes, your face, hear your voice. And don't cheat yourself by upstaging yourself during audition. Play towards the auditors. You only have a couple of minutes, don't waste a second of it with your back to them.

One thing I've seen actors do which does not work is placing an empty chair where the other character is supposed to be sitting in the scene. They then start talking to the empty chair. Don't do that, it doesn't work and only looks silly.

You should place your imaginary other character either down stage center, downstage right or downstage left. You'll want to keep them at eye level. I've seen actors talking to imaginary characters that seem to be less than two feet tall. Remember, we'll be watching your eyes. If they're looking down towards the floor, that's where we'll assume the other person is supposed to be.

To Sit Or Not Sit During The Monologue Audition.

Most auditions provide a chair that the actor has the option of using during their audition. Please note I said "the option of using." A great many actors use the chair even if the material that they are performing doesn't require them to be seated. Being seated makes actors feel grounded, safe, in control. I've seen actors do monologues where the character is totally out of control, having an emotional tirade, but for some reason, the actor has chosen to remain seated for the entire audition.

What determines whether you should be seated or not? The answer quite simply is the material that you're auditioning with. If the monologue takes place at a table in a restaurant where you're conversing with someone at the table, obviously you should be seated. If it's a high energy, say, relationship-ending monologue, where one person is leaving their spouse, how can you stay in your seat? For some monologues the character might start out being seated and then get up and move around.

When you first start out working on a new monologue, it's perfectly okay to be seated for the first table-reads. But as you progress, *if it feels natural* get up, move about, try things. The only thing you don't want to ever do is upstage yourself while your speaking. Make sure that the auditors at the audition can see you.

I've recently heard that some casting directors are now not providing chairs at auditions. Aware that it's a crutch for many actors, they want to see how the actor deals with not having one. If you find yourself auditioning for one of these casting directors you're going to have to quickly make an adjustment and be able to justify it. One way to deal with this in advance is to spend some time at one of your rehearsals with a plan B, where even though the monologue should be a seated one, you can justify a way to turn it into a standing one.

Setting It "Too Tightly."

We've all experienced those auditions where we delivered the monologue *exactly* as we rehearsed it. Every phrase, every movement, every moment performed just as we had worked on it home. We left the audition room feeling somewhat successful because we did indeed hit every mark. But somewhere inside of us there was a feeling that perhaps we were too safe, maybe we were just too over-rehearsed. We performed "too tightly".

Then there are those other auditions, where, (perhaps by accident) we threw ourselves completely into the material, felt it wholeheartedly. The material went to a whole other place. Our work was more meaningful, richer, deeper, and most of all, more *spontaneous*. It seemed like we discovered something about the character (and ourselves) that we never up knew existed.

What Casting Directors Are Looking For.

Casting directors are looking for confident actors who enter with a sense of self and take charge of their auditions.

They want to see actors that are both friendly and professional. You must give them the impression that you really want to be there. So many actors sort of slither on the stage and look uncomfortable for the entire audition. You must give them the impression that that audition stage is as comfortable as your room at home.

Attitude is a very important part of an audition. I've been at auditions where the actor gives a brilliant performance of their monologue but doesn't have a clue as to how to present themselves afterwards. If an actor comes across as too needy or hostile or too insecure a red flag goes up.

You've got to remember that the monologue audition is a five minute job interview. *Everything counts.* You're being judged not just on your talent but also on how and who you are.

The director is asking himself, *"Can I work with this person?"* The producer is asking himself, *"Can I bank on this person"* The playwright is asking himself *"Will this actor be able to perform the role?"* Everyone in the creative team has their own insecurities, their own agenda. Part of your job is to make them all feel that you're not going to be a problem for them in their production. You must come across as confident, accessible and professional. They don't want to work with actors who put out a negative attitude, would you?

The Steps to A Successful Monologue Audition.

The first step actually begins before the actual audition. Before you leave home in the morning try to get yourself in the right frame of mind. Relax, perhaps do some breathing and stretching. Many actors I know begin their day using visualization techniques to imagine what they would like to happen at the audition.

You should arrive at your auditions at least twenty minutes before your assigned time. You should be friendly and professional to the person who greets you. Even though you may feel nervous, try to remain calm. Don't waste valuable time chatting with other actors or socializing. Once you've settled down, go off in a corner somewhere and begin to relax again. It's always helpful to go off somewhere and silently do a quick speed through of the lines in the monologue. Next do a run through of the piece(s). This should be done softly and shouldn't be performed all out; save that for the audition.

There are two faces that you must be able to show at every audition. The first face is on you when you enter the audition room, it's your professional face. This is the friendly, confident face that tells them that you are a capable and reliable actor. You shouldn't "enter in character." Smile directly at the people auditioning you and say hello. You should always be totally professional, even if you've auditioned for them a dozen times. You should not approach the auditors and shake their hands unless they indicate that they want you to. Many casting directors feel uncomfortable when actors invade their space or may be germaphobes. If you have to hand them your picture and resume, do it quickly and efficiently, and then immediately go to your playing area and prepare to perform your monologue.

You should never begin your monologue until you've arrived at your playing area and have announced what the monologue is from.

When you get to your playing area say your name clearly and then the name of the play that your monologue is from. If the monologue is not from a play, state the source material as clearly as possible. There is no reason to give a description of where in the play the monologue takes place. You don't need to set up the scene.

If you are performing two monologues for the auditions I recommend introducing both at the beginning. That way you can easily glide from one character right into the next without having to return to yourself (the actor).

Now, give yourself a moment, and then allow the *second face* to be revealed. If you've done your preparation well in the waiting area, this face will be just beneath the professional face that you entered with. It is the face, the persona, the mask of your character in the first monologue.

After you've given yourself one last moment (to be certain that you're centered and ready to begin), start your monologue. Take your time, don't rush, and *don't forget to breathe* during the audition. In an attempt to maintain control many actors forget to breathe during auditions. Breathe fully, breathe life into your character.

When you've completed performing the monologue, if they've requested a second one, prepare to make the transition from the first character to the second. Make sure the transition is clean (and should be well rehearsed at home prior to the audition). Complete the first monologue, hold the moment, and then by a slight body movement, perhaps a turning of the head, or perhaps by walking to a nearby spot, prepare to begin the next monologue.

Once again, give yourself a moment before you begin. Take your time, don't rush,—and breathe.

After you've finished the monologue, take a moment, then make eye contact with the auditors again, smile and let them know that you're through.

It's appropriate at this time to say "Thank you." Try not to look into look into their eyes for any kind of approval. Maintain your composure and professionalism. You now have your professional face back on.

If they wish to talk with you, you must be prepared to stay and talk with them. The reason that they might be asking you to stay is that you've given a good audition and they may want to know you a little better, perhaps to see if you're the right person for their play. They may ask you the "So what have you been up to lately?" question. Hopefully you've prepared the answer to this question in advance and are ready to tell them a bit about yourself. Your demeanor should be relaxed, professional and friendly.

When they've finished talking with you, tell them it was great meeting them and leave in a confident, unhurried, professional manner. Once you leave the room, the only thing left to do is to let go of that audition and move on to the next part of your day.

Guide To The Monologues Ratings

The following ratings are based on the Motion Pictures Of America movie ratings. In the case of the monologues they apply to the suggested ages actors should be performing the particular monologue.

G RATING—contains nothing in it's theme or language that deals with sex, violence or any "adult matters." Anyone from children to adults can performed these monologues.

PG RATING—Some of the themes or language may imply sexual or "adult" themes, but is in no way is offensive. It can be performed by teens and adults of all ages.

R RATING—These monologues have adult themes and adult language. They should not be performed by anyone under 18.

Age/Age Range Of The Characters

The characters age (or the playing age range) of each character as well is listed directly beneath the characters name, at the top of the page. These are merely suggestions. In some cases, if you wish, you can do a monologue where the age suggested is older or younger.

Genre Of The Monolgue

The genre indicates whether the monologue is comedic, dramatic or serio-comedic. Occasionally actors are asked to specifically bring in a comedic or dramatic monologue or two contrasting monologues (generally comedic and dramatic) for their audition. The genre can be found under the characters name.

Running Time

For many years actors were asked to bring in a "short" monologue or a monologue that was "two minutes and under." Today, one-minute monologues are being requested more often than before. This book has monologues of all lengths. To help you select by time, I've indicated the approximate running time of each piece below the characters name. These times are not set in stone, since every actor has their own speaking rate. I've purposely included many one-minute monologues in this book, as they are being requested more often these days.

Synopsis of Each Monologue

Whether the monologue is from one of my plays or an original monologue, I've provided some brief background information for each monologue.

These are just suggestions where each monologue would be most effective as an audition piece. Subject matter, physical requirements, and intensity are some of the considerations I took into account when determining where the monologue would be most effective. You'll notice many monologues will be effective in several of the listed audition spaces. Once again, these are just suggestions. If you feel a piece can be performed in a venue not suggested, try it out.

THEATER—These monologues work best for theater auditions, theater company auditions, and theater conference auditions.

AGENTS OFFICE—These intimate monologues can be performed in an agents office. They also work being seated directly opposite the agent at their desk in the office.

T.V. AND FILM—These monologues work best for those auditions where you are asked to bring in a short monologue. Don't play directly to the lens, look to the side of the lens or to the person running the camera (unless you are specifically asked to "play to camera"). Be aware of your volume and playing level. Generally less is more, but your truth (acting honesty) still remains the same. Much of what the camera reveals to the audience is the truth in your eyes.

CLASSROOM MONOLOGUES—These are monologues that generally are a bit longer than audition monologues. They may not be necessarily a role the actor would be cast in but they offer the actor material to stretch in acting classes. They may be more emotionally demanding than audition monologues or require more of a physical life.

Part Two

WOMEN'S MONOLOGUES

MARGO

Comedic
mid twenties to forties
G
All venues

Margo fantasizes about seeing and being Julia Roberts.

Running Time: 2 minutes

I'm in the mood to see a Julia Roberts movie. Something light, uplifting—to get me out of this *mood.* A romantic comedy; where Julia always gets the guy. The guy who makes his move early on in the movie. But Julia resists him. Teases, tells him, *(coyly)* "No, you're nice, but I'm not interested." She can say that, cause, well, she's Julia Roberts! Can turn guys down left and right. Make them realize that if they r*eally* want her, they'll have to work very hard to win her love.

And so the guy will pursue her for the rest of the movie. And each time he tries to get too close, she'll say *(A little more forceful, but still very coy)* "Please, just leave me alone. I'm not interested, *really!"*

(Getting revved up) But inside, inside, Julia will secretly enjoy that look of *rejection* on his face. Because that rejection will make him work harder and harder to win my, uh, Julia's love. To beg for me, I mean, Julia, *Julia*! See, I can say or do anything I want in the movie, 'cause, well, hell, I'm *Julia Roberts!* I've got great teeth, a killer smile and I'm smart! And I know, know how to put men through hoops! How to torment, *torture*! Make them suffer endless . . . ! *(Stopping, realizing)* —Wait a minute, hold on; I don't want to be Julia Roberts. I don't *need* to play those silly games with men. I'm better than that. I want to *dominate*; make men beg! Not be just some "girl" that "assholes" can take advantage of; never call back. Ignore! (*Getting all revved up)* Not Julia, no. I want

. . . I want to be SIGOURNEY WEAVER! THAT'S who I want to be! To hell with Julia! I want to beat the crap out of Aliens and belittle weak-minded men who don't "appreciate" who I am or what I'm worth. You don't mess with—Sigourney! Or she'll kick your ass from here to there! She'll open your chest with my bare hands and—rip your heart right out! What was I thinking?! Julia Roberts, whatta wimp! Sigourney doesn't take crap from anyone! She doesn't have to wait for phone calls from men who *never* call back! She doesn't need too! She's—SIGOURNEY-WEAVER—Yeah, Sigourney! SIGOURNEY, THAT'S WHO I WANT TO BE!

JANIE

Dramatic
Teenage to any age
G
All venues

Janie recalls bedtimes with her grandfather as a child.

Running Time: 1 minute, 10 seconds

(A tender memory, softly)

Grandpa got so old, so fast. Remember when we were kids and we'd play Ring-a-round a rosie with him? So much fun.

"Ring-a-round a rosie.

A pocket full of posies.

Ashes! Ashes!

We all fall down!"

But then that day, grandpa did. He fell. Down those stairs, hurt his hip so bad; had to stay in bed. Was in that bed for so long. Seemed like forever. He got so old, so fast. Stopped smiling, playing . . . . I miss him, still, I do. Don't you? He was . . . ! Grandpa was so . . . ! Ya know, sometimes he comes to me in my dreams, he does. But in my dreams he's just like he was before he fell. All smiles and laughs and full of life! And you're there too, and we're all having such a good time, just like we use to. And in my dream, we're playing Ring-a-round a rosie. But what's funny is, I always wake up right before grandpa says "We all fall down." He never says it; not in my dreams, no. Maybe that's why when I wake up, I'm always—smiling.

JENNIFER

Comedic
thirties to fifties
PG
All venues

*Jennifer explodes after her husband deserts her for a
younger woman.*

Running Time: 1 minute, 40 seconds

I hate him. Hate her. Hate them! Hate 'em all, all of 'em!
And my kids, they knew, yeah, knew all along. They knew
and never told me! And I gave birth to those little bastards.
Breast feed 'em. Sat with them through measles and mumps.
And *this* is how they repay me. To favor *her* over me?! I'll
tell you something, revenge is a soup you don't have to stir.
Just light a flame and it cooks itself.

Revenge. And so I went to the bank this afternoon, emptied out our accounts, *all our accounts; every penny.* Made
sure he won't have pot to piss in. Let's see how much she
wants him when she finds out he's broke. Emptied the vaults,
got all my jewelry, sold the car, left. Revenge.

(A beat)

You're a good listener, much better than him, believe
me. I know, sometimes I talk too much. 'Specially when I
get excited like this.

So, anyway—I want a ticket. No, I want a lot of tickets!
I want to go everywhere, you understand?! Wherever your
airline flies, I wanna go. This is my first time leaving New
York, yeah. Been too busy being a wife, a mom, a doormat.
But now the door is open and I am so outta here! I want you
to sell me tickets to EVERYWHERE! Europe, Egypt, Vegas.
I got a Platinum Amex, no limits. Buy, bye, bye. World's
my oyster, and I'm gonna see the sights. Want to see what I

been missin' all these years. Help me, Miss. Help me decide. Money's no . . . . As many tickets as that machine can print. You just keep 'em comin'! And all of 'em, all of 'em, one way, no return. I have a passport! Show me the world, Miss. One way, no return—Revenge.

LYLA

Dramatic
thirties to forties
PG
Film, TV, Classroom. Agent

Lyla talks about the unusual seduction she does in bars.

Running Time: 3 minutes 20 seconds

(Gently, softly)

I always know them. Well, I can usually spot them, right away. It's like a sixth sense or something. They're usually the ones talking too loud, making with the jokes, laughing too loud. Talking; talking to . . . whoever's around, next to them, next bar stool. Maybe their friends, maybe not. Maybe they're people they just met, I don't know, doesn't matter. So I sit, and wait, and watch. I want to be sure.

—I like bars that are bars, not clubs or lounges. Just good old-fashioned *drink bars* where people can sit and talk and hear. And the lighting's usually dim, and the music's not too loud.

So soon I'll have a drink or two to loosen up. As I continue to watch them. I need to be certain. By now I know all the signs.

As the night goes on, they get louder and their laughter . . . It's usually around then that I mosey over, get closer, a bar stool nearby. Let them see me, know I'm there. By now they're up on their drinks and are very accepting of all new friends. And so I ingratiate myself, let them know I think they're funny; as I laugh at their unfunny jokes. As the drinks keep coming.

And soon, well sooner rather than later, the two of us become engaged in some frivolous conversation about . . . . doesn't t matter. So I suggest that we move away from the bar, somewhere quieter. "Sure", they'll say. And we do.

Perhaps to a darkened corner somewhere, or maybe a small out of the way table. And soon, somewhere in that shadow, I look into their eyes and ask, *(Very softly, caring)* "So, . . . what's going on?" Perhaps it's how I say it; like I mean it, like I really want to know. Because usually at that moment, their expression changes. They look at me as if . . . as if for the very first time. I mean here we've been talking . . . And so I say it again, *(Softly, sincerely)* "What; what's going on? Tell me." Then there is that moment where the tide changes, where the curtain opens. Where everything is different than it was just a moment before. And then they talk, begin *really* talking; but now their voice is much softer.

(A beat)

Sometimes . . . sometimes it's about grief. Sometimes, it's about the end of a long love affair or a marriage that ended. Or sometimes it's about something that happened a long time ago—something that still haunts them. But it always seems to be about loss. Pain. And then they talk, and talk and talk. But they usually speak very softly. —And then they cry; almost always. And sometimes I cry with them. Maybe even hold their hand. Finally . . . I feel. Finally I feel what . . . !

(A beat)

And sometimes they make these small childlike sounds. Not words, but sounds. And I sit there, and listen, and let them know I'm there. Because in that moment, I care—very much. We are not strangers anymore. And we both sit there until, well, there's nothing more to say, so we're silent for a while. There's just bar noise and music. And perhaps someone else laughing too loud at the bar. And I know it's time for me to go. And I do; without much fanfare. Sometimes I tell them my name, my first name. And sometimes I don't. I just leave, smile, say good night, wish them the best. And then I go . . . home.

um...   fifties
G
All venues

Emily tells her mother about a man she recently met.

Running Time: 1 minute 10 seconds

Mom, how can you be so mean, how can you say that? You don't know how many nights . . . I'd finally come to the conclusion, okay, s'just the way it is; get use to it. Some women just don't meet their uh, whatever. Maybe I was too choosy or—scared, I don't know. All I knew was that there was no one out there for me. Then last month, like out of the blue . . . I was standing there, waiting by that bus stop. I mean I never in a million . . . —He loves me ma, he does! And he needs me, and I *need him,* yeah. Everything doesn't always have to be picture perfect. And no, I'm not *settling*! You know nothing about him! All you know . . . All you saw was a man in a wheel chair who can't walk; and you come to conclusions. Feel sorry for him. Well don't, I don't! I see someone who's vital, alive! Someone who really loves me. And that's it, that's all. That's all that really matters, ma!

Can't you just be happy for me, huh? This once. I'm in love! Your daughter is in love. And I am so happy. Can't you be happy for me?

CAMILLE

Comedic
thirties to forties
PG
All venues

*Here Camille tells a close friend of a terrible relationship
she recently was involved in.*

Running Time: 1 minute 35 seconds

(Upset, emotional, a tirade)

Mendacity! I mean, who uses words like that?! Who?!
Actors; actors do. Well he did, Alan did. What was *I thinking*?! There can only be one drama queen in a bed, Barbara.
And I had three; him, me and Tennessee Williams. What-the-
hell-was-I-thinking?!

I mean you meet a man at a play, find out he's an actor,
and you should run, right? Run! But what do I do? Went out
with him for dinner. Why? Well, main reason was I realized
he was straight. Attractive, straight?! How many single, attractive, straight men do you meet at a musical-comedy on
Broadway, huh Barbara? VERY, VERY FEW! So I thought,
maybe this one's different, a *sensitive, together,* straight man.
But that's an oxymoron, and I was a moron for even thinking
it! He told me he wanted to be Brick to my Maggie. And I
thought, Brick, Maggie, weren't they miserable? That was
the first clue. Thought I could *change him*, make him not be
so god-damn *needy.* But he's an actor, they all are! Within a
month I was his mommy. Within six months I was his shrink.
Needy, NEEDY! Finally I couldn't take it anymore, so I just
kicked him the hell out. Told him— " I'm sorry, it's me, not
you!" That's when he started yelling it, "Mendacity! Mendacity!" I'm telling you, he got crazy; certifiable! —Barbara,
I'll never get involved with another actor again!

Anyway, last I heard, he was in some pathetic play, down town. I mean down, down town, under a bridge or in an alley or something. He called, asked me if I'd come see him in it. Told him " I would rather die a thousand deaths." I know, that was very harsh; I coulda been kinder. But I just didn't want to hear him yelling that word "Mendacity!" again. Figured I'd just tell him the cold truth. And now I have made a firm commitment Barbara, I will never, ever get involved with an actor again. Matter of fact, I've decided to never even go to the theater ever again; so ha!

ANNIE

Dramatic
Any age
G
All venues

Annie tenderly recalls her mother. Here, she shares some of those memories with her daughter.

Running Time: 1 minute 40 seconds

I remember when I was a little girl, about to fall sleep. My momma'd come to my room, every night, sit on my bed, hold me, tell me my bed time stories. Just like I do with you. And I'd listen to her voice, so soothing, as I'd slowly leave one world and gently drift off into another. Till I went to dreamland, the Feather Ball. I'd been afraid of the dark ever since my daddy died. But momma being there every night, well . . .

One time, momma, she got me this lamp for my room. Had a soft light, and when you turned it on, the lampshade would turn real slow; like magic. And then there'd be make believe clowns and animals all over my walls and ceiling. Movin' in like a slow soothing circus. And sometimes momma would tell me stories about each and every one of them. God how I loved that lamp and the magic it bestowed.

(A beat) Then, well, after momma died, was no one there to hold me at night. Grandma and grandpa . . . just wasn't the same. And I'd have these nightmares, all the time. Dreams of me being pulled out of momma's arms into the night sky. And I'd be screaming for her as I went higher and higher into the dark And grandma, she'd hear me screaming in my room and would come running in. Tell me how it was just a nightmare, and that everything was okay; was just a dream. And she'd turn on my lamp and I'd see my circus on the ceiling and think about momma and her stories. And the memories

of the Feather Ball; my magic place far away. Where feathers always fell and were soft and soothing. And pretty soon I'd fall back asleep; remembering, smiling, remembering.

WENDY (FROM *SOMETHING SEEN, SOMETHING SAID*)

Dramatic
G
Adult
All venues

*Wendy tells her husband about a woman that she encoun-
tered earlier who may or may not have been dead.*

Running Time: 1 minute 30 seconds

It was a strange turn of events. I mean she was just
sitting there, alone, this lady. Shopping bags, pocketbook
by her chair, looked like anyone else there. Starbucks, the
one on Forty-Second near Eighth. I ordered a coffee, was
sitting, and I saw her and . . . something seemed I don't
know, wrong. Her head was like tilted. She was like lean-
ing over, sitting there in that chair, her head . . . Well, she
looked like she was dead. Everyone else there was just
walking by. No one even noticed. New York, right? People
can be so insensitive!

And I noticed there was like *saliva* dripping out of the
side of her mouth. Yeah, like large drops, just dripping.
She certainly seemed dead. 'Mean I didn't take her pulse
or anything. But you can't tell, y'know. I noticed that her
skin, the color; pale, almost *yellow.* I decided then she was
definitely *dead.*

(A beat. Then, softly)

Her name was Alison Courter. She lives on East 52nd
street; or lived. Had a husband, couple of kids; well they
looked like teenagers. Hard to tell from the photograph.—
The photographs that were in her . . . Well, I . . . took her
pocketbook. 'Mean she didn't need it anymore, right?! And
inside there was money. My God, so much money! And credit
cards that I used immediately to buy things. Things we've

needed . . . . Well she was dead! And we're out of work. And why not, y'know? Who was hurt? There it was, a gift. AND WHY THE HELL NOT?!

TERRY (FROM *AFTER*)

Serio-comedic
PG
late forties to late sixties
All venues

After discovering that a man she just met is gay, Terry tells him about the great love of her a life, her husband; who was also gay.

Running Time: 1 minute 15 seconds

My husband was gay too, like you. Gay as a goose-whatever that means. And we were married, Sidney and me, nearly thirty-two years. And let me tell you, you couldn't ask for a better husband. We never talked about it, his being gay, but he knew I knew. A *wink* every once in a while. Times were different back then. No need to talk about things like that. 'Sides why ruin a good thing, right? And let me tell ya, I loved being his wife. Everyday with Sidney was a blessing. He was a good, caring man. Anyway, I feel people talk too much today. Talking's overrated. I hated Oprah and now all those stupid talk shows. People always needing to reveal every . . . ! Sometimes what really matters . . . It's the *not saying*, y'know? The things people don't need to say to each other. The, I don't know, *unspoken,* that's most meaningful. Sidney was more than just my husband, he was my *companion*. Friends and lovers, eh, they come and go. But a *companion*, that's someone *special.*

YETTA (FROM *COULDA, WOULDA, SHOULDA*)

Comedic
PG
Adult
All venues for performance

*Yetta tells her husband about an odd event that happened
earlier that day while giving her young son a bath.*

Running Time: 1 Minute

That's what he said! This morning when I gave him his
bath. What a kid, could you bust? Stood up in the tub, put his
hand on my shoulder and said, "Ma, I want to be a rabbi!"
At first I thought he said, "rabbit." Yeah, thought he said,
"Ma, I want to be a rabbit." Almost dropped the sponge I
laughed so hard. I mean can you imagine? But then he looked
at me, seemed so serious. You know those eyes of his? Said
it again, loud and clear, black and white. Looked like a little
Moses in the tub waiting for the waters to part. (Slowly, very
strong) "Ma, I want to be a rabbi, a rabbi, you understand?!"
I stopped, smiled, what could I . . . ? Said, "Sure, okay, if
that's what you want. Washed the soap off, towel-dried him,
baby powder, kissed him on the head and gave him a big
hug. But then he gave me a look, got upset, started to cry. I
don't know why. I asked him, wouldn't answer. Looked at
me like I was the worst mother in the world. Then he ran to
his room, slammed the door, locked it shut. Wouldn't let me
in. Couldn't get him out. Been in there all morning.

PAMELA (FROM *THE PAIN IN THE POETRY*)

Comedy
thirties and older
G
Theater

After finding out that her husband has secretly been writing a play for two years, she reveals that she's been secretly writing poetry.

Running Time: 45 seconds

It's . . . it's a poem! I've been writing poetry, okay?! What was I supposed to do, knit all day?! I had to do something! You were always away, or upstairs locked in the bathroom writing your play. I was going out of my mind with loneliness. Then one day in my despair, a couplet came to me. A rhyme, and then a verse. A beautiful image, a matching thought. And after that, well, there was no stopping me. I never told you about my poems because, well, you were never here. And when you were, you were always a million miles away, probably thinking about your *precious play*. *(Gently)* And my poems, they kept me company, gave me such solace. My poetry was something I didn't have to share with anyone. They were mine alone; mine alone. So yes, I admit it, I-am-a-poet.

KATHLEEN

Serio-comedic
twenties to fifties
PG
Film, TV, Classroom. Agent

Kathleen recalls a terrifying experience she had on a subway.

Running Time: 2 minutes 50 seconds

You know me, I'm not like that. But that's what happened, yeah. I was sitting there on the subway, express train, uptown. Was just the two of us, her right across from me. Air conditioning was off, so it was very hot. She had this sweet face; young, maybe seventeen. She seemed upset. And you know me, I don't usually . . . Well I went over, said, "You okay, miss? She spoke Spanish, didn't understand me. Pointed to her belly. She was wearing a big blouse. Thought she was just "overweight." I didn't realize . . . And then Brenda, things started to happen very fast She started to scream, yeah, all of a sudden. There was no one else in the car, I didn't know what to do. And then—it happened. Her water broke! I started to scream. 'MEAN I HAD NO IDEA WHAT TO DO!'

(Starts getting revved up) I helped her lie down on the . . . Then all this stuff, blood, water . . . 'Mean I'd seen it in movies, on TV. I told her to breathe, BREATHE! But realized she didn't speak . . . So I started breathing, pushing air through my lips. *(SHE does)*. Said, "BREATHE! C'mon, BREATHE!" She started breathing, blowing threw her lips. Subway was just wizing by the stations. I told her, PUSH, c'mon, PUSH; YOU CAN DO IT!! Was like I'd seen them do on *Greys Anatomy*. "PUSH! PUSH! Then she started pushing, yeah! Then . . . I saw it, the baby's head. The tip . . . I could see it! PUSH! PUSH-HARD, NOW! Felt like

a doctor or something. And then in almost an instant, it slid out, this baby, a boy. Slid right out of her—into my hands. I was holding her brand-new-baby!

The train started slowing down, coming into a station. I sat there holding this woman's baby. And I remembered from TV, you gotta cut the cord. So I cut it with my keys, the *ubilical cord*. She started like crying, laughing. Then me too, laughing like lunatics; the two of us!

Train stopped at the station. People entered the car, saw us. Some came running. "It's her baby; she just had it!, I said like an idiot. People came over, helped; especially the women. Someone pulled the emergency cord. Why hadn't I thought of that? In a heart beat the cops came. In a minute, the medics were there. I sat there, numb, covered with this woman's blood. She looked at me, as the medics came, took her away. Maybe I should have gone with . . . Think I was in shock. Gave her a big thumbs up! And she gave me the biggest thumbs up ever and a smile. Then she was gone. I sat there, just shaking. Some people were still staring at me, smiling. Felt so good.

Subway doors closed; subway started up again.
(A beat, softly) I helped deliver a baby, Brenda. I did that-today. I did . . . I did.

CLAIRE

Dramatic
forties to sixties
R
All audition venues

Claire meets with her daughter for the first time since she was an infant.

Running Time: 1 minute 15 seconds

Like hers, yeah. You have 'em; my mother's eyes. Just like hers. I look at you and . . . Mothers, hm.

Heard you put a lot of time into this. S'been like, what, your whole life's obsession or somethin'? Well now you found me, seen me, heard me; so? I know you're probably hopin' this'll be like in some sentimental movie. Y'know, with the music, and hugs; us making future plans. Holiday get-togethers. *(Staring at her)* Sorry, ain't gonna happen.

Yeah; you got my mothers eyes but you also got *his skin.* You remind me of him. Of that night. And—YOU HAVE NO FUCKIN' IDEA! You are nothing but a reminder! A memory of a terri . . . ! Right now, I just wanna tear your eyes out!

(A beat, softer) I'm sorry; but I had to say it. S'just how I feel. I can not forget. There will be no . . . You wasted your time coming here. Go back—to your own family. You found me. Now go find yourself another mother. —This one's already taken.

PAMELA (FROM *THE PAIN IN THE POETRY*)

Comedic
PG
thirties and older
Theater.

> *Pamela has just learned that her husband has secretly been writing a play for two years. Now he tells her that he's thinking of starting a new play. This enrages Pamela.*

Running time: 45 seconds

What's next, huh?! A comedy, some cheap comedy? You're kidding right?! That what you're going to write; a comedy? Oh I can just see it now, you and your *dirty little comedy*. The two of you having lots of laughs in some dark stairwell together. A chuckle on the bathroom floor. Dirty jokes, pathetic puns. Well I'm telling you, the fun's over.

Or is it a musical, huh? That what you're thinking about writing next, a MUSICAL?! Well, let me tell you, I will not play second fiddle to some musical! You are on your own, I am out of here! I'm leaving you, understand?! You . . . you—playwright!

HELEN (FROM *THE HIGH LOW LIFE*)

Dramatic
PG
twenties to forties
Film and TV, Agent, Classroom

*Helen shares how she came to have a nervous breakdown
and what happened after.*

Running Time: 2 minutes, 30 seconds

I was in my small, crappy room on the lower east side. Was watching TV. Hadn't been out in days. Had just moved here to the city, didn't know anyone really. Well maybe the mailman. But he never had any mail for me. Anyway, I don't remember what show was on TV that night. Some police drama I think. And that's when it began. It started with their lips. Yeah, lips. I was watching his mouth move, the character, the actor, but it seemed like the words coming out weren't in synch. His mouth was moving, but the words, his lips . . . Suddenly I started getting real anxious. I couldn't seem to follow the story anymore. It seemed like all of them, all the other characters, them too, their lips were moving, but their words weren't connected; not coming outta their mouths. I started getting like *really* nervous! Tried calming myself, to FOCUS on their lips, their words. But it was out of synch! I started breathing real hard! Thought, I just need to calm down; this is crazy! But whenever I'd looked at the TV, it was all just babble. I became terrified, ran from my room, out into the night, the street. Found a bar a block away. Went in, asked the bartender for a drink, something STRONG! But when he talked, the bartender, his lips, his lips were not in synch with his words! Couldn't understand what he was saying! He started looking at me really weird. I like freaked, left. Ran outside. Cold. Wind. Ran for blocks and blocks!

Traffic, streetlights, people looking at me like I was a lunatic! Just ran and ran, until I saw a hospital, the emergency room sign. Ran in, saw the woman behind the admissions window. She asked me something, but then her too, her lips . . . Her words . . . ! Finally I just blurted out . . . *(Anxiously, a loud whisper)* "I think I'm having a nervous breakdown!" She looked at me, said, "What?"

(A bit bolder, louder)

"I said, I think I'm having a nervous-breakdown!"

"Can't hear you honey; the partition. Ya gotta speak a little louder"

(Angrily, yelling) " I'M HAVING A GOD DAMNED NERVOUS BREAKDOWN!"

Everyone in the emergency room, the bloodied, injured people who'd been crying, all like stopped, stared. Everyone, everything stopped! Was like a bright spotlight was shining on me.

(The admissions lady, matter of fact) "Nervous breakdown, ya said?"

(Very matter of fact) "Have a seat."

I sat down, put my head down between my knees, waited.

When I saw the doctor, he calmed me down, gave me something to relax. Told me it was just an anxiety attack. Happens, he said. Moving to a big city, not knowing anyone. No family or friends. He wished me well, I went on my way. Back to my dumpy furnished room; cried, slept.

(A beat) I met Carl at a bar in the Bouwerie. Musta been, I dunno, a few days later. I was pretty drunk. When he saw me he asked me . . . *(smiling)* asked me if I was Jesus. He wanted to know if I'd come there to that bar, that night to save him. Please, could I save him? I looked at him, smiled, said, *(softly)* "Yes; yes."

NELL (FROM *THE BAGELS AND BRUNCH SCENE- REVISED*)

Serio-comedic
mid-twenties on up
PG
All venues

*Fed up with what she sees as her husbands mind games,
Nell lashes out at him.*

Running Time: 55 seconds

How could you be so mean? Huh, how could you?! I *know* what you meant just now. I *know* what you were really trying to say, okay?! I know that when you say things sometimes, like you did just now, you actually mean the *opposite.* Yeah! You choose your words, dress 'em up, try to make 'em sound good. And then BAM! The hit, the hurt, the hammer to my head! It's abusive what you just said! And I knew it was coming. Oh, I knew! Yeah! I've been here before, many times. It's like clockwork, tic-toc, the cat waiting for the canary to drop the cheese. Just had to wait, that's all. Just sit here, sip my coffee, and sift through your usual Sunday morning *verbiage.* I-know-you Ned. I know you, and I am so on to you!

G WYNN

Dramatic
thirties to 60
R
All venues

After a tragic event, Gwynn is sitting on the front porch or her house, talking to a neighbor. She's strong, speaks her mind.

Running Time: 1 minute 15 seconds

Garry's got a gun. He's back in the back bedroom with the kids. S'my turn out here. Looks like we got a nice night though, y'know? Not too cold, no *rain*. Got some nice moon up there, right? But it's sure as shit's quiet, right? . . . Who'd ever have thought, y'know? S'crazy. Life; shit. Was what, just last week, you and me sittin' out here, shootin' the breeze, talkin' about sales, the kids. You could hear the neighbors yellin', the TV's, cars racing. Nice; normal. But now—shit, look at this. ONE STUPID STORM AND BOOM! LOOKS LIKE A GODDAMNED TOILET BOWL OUT THERE; AM I RIGHT?! SHIT! LOOK AT IT!

(A beat. Calming down)

Heard they broke into the Adlers yesterday; yeah. Got their TV's, computers, everything. Third-house-this-week; god-damned looters!

We may have no electricity or water, but thank God we got these *guns*. And Gary, he's got an itchy finger. Just waitin' for them bastards to give him an excuse! He'd be out here so fast, wouldn't think twice. They best not try comin' to my house tonight. They best not try. Not while I'm here, . . . and not while Gary's got that gun.

Anna angrily tells off a man who has just told her that he wants to end their long-term relationship.

Running Time: 1 minute

What do you mean?! I *think* you just said, "It's *over.*" No, wrong, you said, "I'M *SORRY, it's over!*" Don't want to forget you said, "I'm sorry." You apologized, very polite. *Twelve years* and just like that, screw you, good-bye? Really; REALLY?! Who do you think you're talking to here, your mother?!

Said you've given it a lot of thought?! *(Sarcastically)* Well isn't that nice. It's nice to know your *rash decision* wasn't impulsive or anything. I mean we both know how *impulsive* you get sometimes, Harold! You've got to get a handle on that.

(A beat)

There's someone else, isn't there? Of course.' Of course there is I really don't care. Just go, leave! You're no longer my concern. *(Trying to be civil)* I wish you the best, Harold, really. *(Looking at her watch, dismissive)* You're time's almost up anyway. Just leave the check for this *last* session on the table by the door. And don't look so *lost* as you leave. I have other patients out there who *appreciate what I do for them every session* . . . . Have a good life, Harold. Try hard not to self destruct too much. Try.

DONNA

Comedy
G
thirties to fifties
All venues

Donna, a poor, single mom, has a dream that she's getting a manicure and chatting with the late Princess Diana.

Running Time: 2 minutes

So in my dream, I'm sittin' next to Princess Diana. Princess Diana, yeah! We're both getting a mani-pedi at the palace. And we're sittin' there, talkin' about our kids, ya know. The problems you have bringing up boys, stuff like that. Like what happened with her Harry in Vegas, and me with my Carlos when he got caught stealing that car. And as I'm talking, it dawns on me, *Oh my God, I'm talking to Princess Diana*!! But then I thought, wait, didn't she die, isn't she's dead? So I said "Excuse me, your most royal majesty, but didn't you like pass away?" We looked at each other. God she's beautiful. Love her hair, that style, that little flip she got in the front, so cute.

And the Princess said, "Yes, indeed I'm dead, but it's no big deal."

"No?!"

"Not at all, it's the same up there as it is here."

"It is?"

"They just have more spas, and no one frowns and money is not allowed.

"No?"

"Everything is paid for with a kiss."

"A kiss, no kiddin'. S'no food stamps?"

"No. Nor are there, I'm happy to say, any paparazzi chasing you; because there's no need. *Because everyone is a star.*"

"They are?"

When you get there, you realize you always were, you just didn't know.

"A star, wow, I never thought!" So then I said, "So now that you're in heaven, Princess, are you finally happy? I mean, I read that when you were alive, you had some pretty bad stuff going on, made you miserable. Did you finally find happiness in heaven?"

And just then—I woke up. My nails were digging deep into the sheet; I realized I needed a manicure.

I wondered, did Princess Diana finally find happiness in heaven, I really wanted to know. God, I hope so.

Then I got up, made some coffee, woke Carlos up. Gave him a little kiss on the head.

(Growling) "Hey." he said, "What's that for?! *(Tough, but loving)* "S'for nothing, s'just a kiss for Christ's sake, no big deal; get up!"

Then I went into the kitchen, started his breakfast, looked out the window. Was nice out, sunny. I suddenly had this good feelin' all over'. Felt like, I don't know, like it was gonna be a really nice day.

HELENE (FROM *THE HIGH LOW LIFE*)

Serio-comedic
R
twenties to thirties
All venues

*Fed up with all the stuff her boyfriend has put her through,
Helene tells him what she plans to do.*

Running Time: 1 minute 15 seconds

Miami, you hear me?! I'm going to go to Miami, South
Beach! Where it's hot, and I can lie out in that sun and wear a
bikini bathing suit. Or maybe even a *thong* if I want to! Or if
I really want, I won't wear anything! Go topless, bottomless,
bare ass! Just lie there on that beach, stretch my legs, and
cover myself all over with suntan oil, and watch them rich
old men eyeing me, circling me like vultures. As I soak up
the sun, and pretend I don't notice 'em. Until I decide, till I
deem who the hell I want to go home with. And I'll look up,
smile, and pick the one who looks like he's the wealthiest.
And him I will go home with. I'll go back with him to his
expensive hotel room. And I will have sex with him baby,
lots of sex, for lots and lots of money! And HE will *appreciate* me, *admire* me, desire me. He'll know what I'm worth.
And I'll stay with him in his big ass room at that Art Deco
hotel. Where they got room service, twenty-four, seven. And
I'll enjoy every minute, baby. Know why? Because I won't
have to listen to assholes like you belittling me, day in, day
out. Making me feel like scrap metal. Well I'm GOLD baby,
14 KARAT! And I am leaving you, you hear me? I'm going
to Miami!

YVONNE

Comedic
G
twenties and up
All venues

After seeing her things destroyed, Yvonne, upset, goes on a rampage.

Running Time: 1 minute 40 seconds

(Upset, a tirade)

Why? Why did you do . . . ?! Do you know what you've done here?! All the work I've . . . I'm NUMB! This . . . it's *irreparable,* do you understand?!—Why?! You've sat there, seen me work on this, so you know! YOU KNOW HOW MUCH THIS MEANT TO ME; THIS PROJECT! DON'T LOOK AT ME LIKE THAT! Do you have any idea what my boss is going to . . . ?!

(A beat, softer)

I have gone out of my way, been good to you. Maybe, I don't know, maybe too good. Gave you everything! Put a roof over your . . . DON'T-LOOK-AT-ME-LIKE . . . ! Won't work!

What do you want from me, huh? I come home and see all these pages . . . S'like you tore into them with your *teeth.* MALICIOUS! Do you hate me that much?! I've done everything I could for you! Bought you the best *toys;* the best everything. That rubber duck, c'mon, you *love* that rubber duck. You love how it squeals when you bite . . . How it bounces. Why didn't you just bite your god-damned rubber duck?!

(A beat, exhausted)

No, don't crawl over here. You stay, *stay there.* I want you to think about what you've done here. Mommy is mad.

(A beat)

No, roll back over. That will not work, I'm not . . . ! I will not rub . . . RUB YOUR OWN BELLY!

(Softening)

Don't . . . Don't come over here. —STAY; stay!

(Starting to ease up, a slight smile)

Bad; you're bad; you know that. You made mommy very, very angry,

(Smiling, obviously being taken, over falling for it)

Bad girl, yes you are.

Rolling over won't . . . Stop that.

(Then, totally melted. Waving her over, smiling, lovingly)

Alright. Alright, come over here. Well, do you want your belly rubbed or not? You're bad . . . Come on, . . . come to mommy.

SUE (FROM *SPILT MILK*)

Dramatic
G
late forties to seventies
All venues

*Martha sadly tells her husband Murray about her visit
with her sister at the hospital that day.*

Running Time: 1 minute, 10 seconds

I saw Martha today, Murray. Don't ask. She's the same,
yeah. Same as always. Same as yesterday, day before. No
better, no worse. Just stares up at that ceiling. Lies there in
that hospital bed, and talks . . . talks to I don't know who.
Angels on the ceiling or something. Who the hell knows
who she talks to anymore? Who can even understand her?
Just babbles like a baby . . . . Y'know, maybe she's preparing
Murray. Gettin' ready to go. She just talks an' talks in like
baby talk. A conversation to nobody; thin air! And she don't
know me, no; don't know nobody anymore.

(Slightly hopeful) But I'll tell you Murray, there was a
second today, just a *second*, where from the corner of her
eye I saw like a *glimmer,* y'know? She gave me a look and
it was like old times! I remembered that look from way back
when. For one moment, Murray, I thought hey, maybe she's
gonna snap out of it. Maybe a miracle! Say, "Edna, EDNA,
c'mon, I was just pretendin', foolin' around. S'gonna be
alright! S'gonna be just like old times!" And she'd throw
the blankets back, jump outta bed, and say, "Come on Edna,
let's-go-shopping!" And we'd laugh, grab our bags, an' run
downtown; just like we used to.—

(Then, softly) But . . . was just a look, a look, Murray.
Meant nothing, nothing at all.

STELLA

Serio-comedic
fifties to seventies
G
Film, TV, Classroom, Agent

*Stella recalls the day she mistakenly ended up in a room
with the coffin of a man she idolized.*

Running Time: 2 minutes 10 seconds

I'm not an innocent, I was an actress; but it WAS as accident. Well not so much an accident as . . . I was on the upper East side, dropping off head shots at some casting . . . Anyway I was walking down Madison Avenue, day-dreaming. And this door just opened, and someone walked out. And I have no idea why, but I thought it was the back door to a diner. I was hungry, so I just, I don't know, walked in. A man in a black suit, looking very serious, came over to me and said, "Family?" And I'll never know why, but I lied, said "Yes." I hadn't seen the crowds, I swear, so I had no idea.

Anyway, this man quickly took me to a room, then opened the door. I stood there. He pointed, said, "He's over there." At first I didn't move, didn't know what . . . But then I saw the coffin in the corner. The man in the suit looked at me . . . *compassionately.* So I smiled back, *appreciatively.* Was like I was playing a part in a play. I nodded, entered the room, the smell of flowers almost overwhelming me. I slowly approached the coffin. The door closed; I was alone. The coffin was open. I leaned in, looked. *Oh my God!* I mean I'd heard, I knew, the news, T.V. The Elysee Hotel, drugs, some Seconal. It was . . . Tennessee Williams was in the coffin! TENNESSEE WILLIAMS! His famous line ran through my mind, "I have often depended on the kindness of strangers." I'd ALWAYS wanted to play Blanche. And here was the greatest of great playwrights! And he seemed . . .

so small, almost tiny. I leaned in, wanted just to touch . . . .
Suddenly the door to the room opened. I heard someone yell.
"What are you doing there?! It was the tall man in the suit,
but now he wasn't such a kind stranger anymore. He quickly
grabbed my arm, said, *(Angrily)* "Sorry, you have to leave!"
I think he also said, "Liar!", but I'm not sure. A small group
of people stood at the door, watched me as I was quickly es-
corted outside, to the street. Where there were now hundreds
of people standing on a very long line. I saw the sign, Frank
E Campbell Funeral Chapel. Why hadn't I seen . . . ? Did
that really happen? Was I really in there, with *him?!* Yes, of
course, it did, it happened—a long time ago, when I was a
young actress. The day I *me*t Tennessee Williams . . . . Two
lines come to mind, one last time. "I don't want realism. I
want magic!" Yes, Mr. Williams, I understand . . . *now.*

CHRISTINE

Serio-comedic
thirties to fifties
PG
All venues

Christine, seated in a car with her intoxicated husband, is enraged about what just happened while he was driving.

Running Time: 1 minute 15 seconds

(Upset, a tirade)

No, no it was not! It was not an accident. I was here, right next to you. I almost went through that windshield there! IT WAS NOT AN ACCIDENT!

(A beat) You just had to have it, huh, that one-last-drink with the boys!

I kept saying, *(Softly)* "John, Johnny, c'mon, think we should go. C'mon Johnny, please."

But no, you wouldn't listen, would ya? Had to impress your *friends* at the party. The boys who'd probably stab you in the back for a bump up in the company. They could care less.

Don't pay any attention to the little woman; what does she know? Well, I'll tell ya. I knew, could see, I saw your eyes. I knew you were shit-faced. But-you-wouldn't-listen! Had to be the big man at the party!

—If I'd had my glasses with me , s'no way I would have let you get behind that wheel! But you kept saying, "No, I'm fine; fine!"

(A beat, controlled anger)

You are gonna turn this car around right now, you understand? And we're going to drive back- to the scene of the crime, *real* slow.

I still can't believe you just left it there! You hit, hurt it and left it. Even after we heard it howl . . . It-was-crying! —And if it's alive, that poor thing; if it's still out on the road, you're gonna get it to a vet. I don't care what time it is. 'Cause if you don't, I swear to God I will get on my cell phone and report you to the god-damned police. Hit and run, injured animal. Someone's dog I believe.

—So what's it gonna be, huh, Mr. Coward? You coming, we going, WHAT?!?

HELENA (FROM *TWO LADIES SITTING IN A GARDEN*)

Dramatic
sixties to seventies
PG
All venues

> *Helena, an older gay woman in a nursing home, speaks to her close friend as they sit out in the garden.*

Running Time: 1 minute 8 seconds

(Gently, lovingly) Suffice it to say, Christine could just walk into a room and it was like the windows and doors flew open. All the musty air seemed to empty out. People would turn, look. All eyes would be on her. And she really wasn't really that much of a beauty. Was just who she was, I guess. There was, I don't know, magic. And it never really bothered me if other women looked at her, wanted her. Because I knew she was with me. We were *together; soul mates. (Softly)* And you feel so lucky, blessed! You both live in this lovely *love bubble*. Joy. Great times, special moments, wonderful memories. You wake up every morning and . . . *(Her mood suddenly changes, abruptly, very strong)* No, enough; no more! End of this conversation. They told me not to talk about . . .! *(SHE looks at MARLA)* Too past-tense! Ancient history! I must *stay* in the moment; in THE MOMENT! *(Looking out, a bit manic)* Let's just enjoy this . . . this very beautiful day! Look at it, lovely. Lovely, right?! It's a lovely-god-damned day! The weather, Marla, that's the subject at hand. The weather; let's talk about the god damned weather!

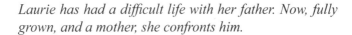

Laurie has had a difficult life with her father. Now, fully grown, and a mother, she confronts him.

Running Time: 1 minute 10 seconds

Dad, don't! Don't dad, please. I'm asking you; warning you! I'll leave and NEVER come back, you understand?! And I'll take my kids, and you'll never see any of us again!

Never understood why momma always got so mad. Wicked Witch Of the West, remember? That's what you always called her. But now she's gone, she escaped, AND YOU DID THAT DAD; YOU!

—Look, I want you to listen, listen *real* good. 'Cause this is the last time I'm going to tell you. —I love you, okay? Love you so much, but this is it, end of the road. I can't bare to look at you like this. I'm embarrassed to say you're my father.

The kids are in the car, waiting. I will not let them see you like this. Now I have to go out there and tell them grandpa's sick again.

So if you want that drink so bad, go ahead. Then have another and another; just like always. And when you're good and hammered, go take a look in the mirror, and toast the dead man holding a glass. (Sadlly, softly) I gotta go. You . . . you do what you . . . I gotta go dad, my kids are waiting.

DEE DEE

Comedic
thirties to fifties
R
All venues

*Dee Dee talks about how she personally identifies with
"The Good Wife."*

Running Time: 1 minute 30 seconds

I am her, and she is me, and we could be sisters. See, I
can make that same look she does on TV; y'know that *cold
stare (SHE does)* Secret's in the eyes, that's the secret. No
one knows what'cha thinkin'. But ya gotta keep it inside,
together, all buttoned up. And I do, just like her. An' yeah,
I know, I don't work for no big fancy law firm, with law
partners and stuff. I work in a small diner. But there's very
little difference between me and her.

Like when I found out my Gianni had a puttana on the
side, some whore he slept with. I sent him packin'; just like
she did with her husband, Peter Floreck. That Peter couldn't
keep his pecker in his pants either. Thought just 'cause he's
some hot shot Attorney General . . . ! Eh, don't get me started;
men, they're all alike!

And just like her, I'm strong, got integrity! *—(Softly,
with guilt)* Okay, there's that one time I *slipped*. But so did
she, with Will Gardner, her law firm partner, in that fancy
hotel, under fancy sheets. (Softer) But with me, it was
with Mike, the short order cook, in the frozen food locker.
But I finally hadda tell him, "No Mike, no more, not like
this—I'm-a-good-wife!" Now me and Mike only give each
other looks of longing, like Alicia and Will. There can be
no more mid day BJ's for Mike, just memories of hot times
and cold meat.

Glenn Alterman 87

And like her husband, my Gianni is also running for office, the plumbers union. And like her I gotta stand by my man! Keep a brave face, just-like-Alicia! We're cut from the same cloth. We are both, both—GOOD WIVES!

STEPHANIE

Serio-comedic
Mid thirties to fifties
PG
All venues

Stephanie warns her sister about the new job she's about to start at a hair salon.

Running Time: 1 minute 50 seconds

No, you can't hate the haters here. As much as it hurts, ya gotta learn to love 'em, or at least let 'em think you do. Listen to me, Marsha, if you play your cards right, they can help you move up fast. Ya gotta let their petty put downs and nasty stares just dissipate, like water off a ducks back. Befriend them, before they *cut you down*. And they will, I've worked here six years, I know. Play the game, be their friend, win customers!

See Sally over there, at the second chair? Now she, her, she's a real *suck up*; tells everyone *anything* they wanna hear. (Very phony) "You look great!" "Did you lose weight" —S'not a sincere bone in her body. Even though her compliments are paper thin, she says 'em with SUCH conviction. People are insecure, she knows it, plays on it. *That's* how she got the *second chair.*

And Bill over there, chair by the door; he can't cut hair for anything. But he lends those large shoulders to his clients to cry on. Mostly gets seniors, the blue hairs. Those old girls *just love* complaining. All their aches and pains and how their families don't miss 'em. He listens with *such concern.* They can't see how badly he cuts their hair; because they're all half blind.

Now Tony and Frido, them, they're the one's you *really* gotta watch out for. The dynamic duo here, the power couple.

If they don't like you, watch out, cause no one else will. Be *extra* nice to them, buy them coffee and doughnuts. Compliment their cuts, especially in front of their customers. You need 'em, Marsha. Without their help you might end up at the back chair in the rear, near the shampoo room, *Siberia*. Ya might as well be cutting hair on the street with a lawnmower if they turn on you.

(A beat) Okay, that's it, end of salon lecture one-on-one. I now bequeath to you my trusty chair. You've wanted it, worked hard, and now it's yours. You're good Marsh, very good. Better with hair than anyone else here. But you gotta PLAY-THE-GAME; pretend to be sincere. I'm telling you sis, their scissors can be weapons. Their dryers can really burn.

MARLA (FROM *TWO LADIES IN A GARDEN*)

Serio-comedic
sixties to seventies
PG
All venues

A lively gay woman in her seventies. She's in a nursing home talking to another gay woman. Fun, full of life.

Running Time: 50 seconds

So I was the go-to-girl for good times! Everyone knew. Well everyone who knew me, knew! And the women that didn't know, well they learned fast, *very fast. (Smiling)* I don't know, I just liked havin' fun back then, that's all. Party-hearty! Have me a couple a shots and . . . Shit, I'd walk into some bar in the village and every woman there knew right off I was seriously out for some *stuff*! I was there for some *take out*! And me, I was kind of a looker back then, had a nice shape too. Did pretty well in them days. Had me a flock of *admirers*! And then one day, with the blink of an eye you're old. The mirror don't lie. And what'cha got left are these memories. And these memories, baby, they're like jewels. You don't want to let go. Well I don't; I never will!

MARYANNE

Serio-comedic
mid twenties to forties
R
All venues

> *Sitting at a window in her living room, taking a break from some "play time" with her boss from work. He enters, she looks at him.*

Running Time: 1 minute, 50 seconds

(She speaks softly, seductively)
Go back to bed, go ahead . . . . I'll be in in a minute . . . . Alright, don't, stand there. Watch me. Gloat. But remember, it's only round one, it's still early.

(A beat) What happened in there just now, and what may or may not happen later is nobody's business; you understand? Cause if you ever talk, and I mean ever, I will walk, leave, go. And you don't want that, know what I mean? It would be very messy. So a word to the wise, hush.

(A beat) Y'know, I had a feeling it might be like this tonight. Even imagined it, yeah. Me out here, you in there; taking a breather between sets. Then both of meeting mid way, toying with the idea of a return engagement. I knew what I was getting into with you. The warnings were all there, but I'm a daredevil. I wanted to see for myself if you were really as good as they say you were. —You're not; sorry. You're too greedy, lack patience. You're even inconsiderate— *(smiling)* and I like that, I do. At times I don't even think you knew I was there. I like that too; feeling invisible. So we're both on the same page. here But the books not finished yet; there's more twists and turns. You're still gloating, good.

Oh I bet you feel like a king, a conqueror, don'cha? I like that too. Keep that gloat, maintain that smug. Turns me on.

—Look, uh, I'm going to go to the bathroom, clean up. I'll meet you back in the bedroom in a few Why don't you go back inside, turn off the light. Get nice and naked. Lay back on the bed. Relax. Wait. Gloat. I'll be right in, soon. And boy oh boy . . . have I got a surprise for you.

CEIL (FROM *The Sealing Of Ceil)*

Dramatic
mid thirties to early sixties
R
All venues

> *After being abused for years by her husband, Ceil, a disturbed woman, finally decides to take matters in her own hand. SHE speaks softly, mostly to herself.*

Running Time: 1 minute 10 seconds

Look at that rain. S'really pouring . . . Ya never really talk to me anymore Mike. Once, yeah. Once ya did, you use to talk to me a lot. But that was a long time ago. Oh how we talked and talked back then, remember? Talked all the time. But now, now; no.

Now you just sit here and yell, and yell And then you go away, on your business trips. And when you come back, you yell some more. You're always yelling at me!

(Looking out the window, and then occasionally to him)

Look at that rain, Mike. They say it's gonna rain all weekend. From Friday to Sunday. Say you'll need an umbrella. Don't forget to take one when you go.

You need an umbrella to protect you. 'Cause you need to be protected, everyone does. Know why? 'Cause when it rains, when it rains like this for so long Mike, you just can't take it anymore. You get so wet. It sort of overwhelms you. You-just-can't-take-it! Feels like it can kill you, that rain.

(SHE looks at him)

So you got to do something. You almost have no choice. It's either you or the rain.

(She has an angry look on her face as she stares at MIKE.)

And the rain won't win. It-won't-win! No . . . . Not anymore.

NAOMI (FROM *THE THINGS THE PLAY*)

Comedic
early twenties to forties
G
All venues

> *Naomi is being investigated for the disappearance of
> all the words from a script of a playwright she knows.*

Running Time: 1 minute 15 seconds

Can you can you please get that light out of my face?!
. . . Thank you. —Alright, so I was at my temp job when the
phone rang. Was Rob, he sounded well, *frantic.* Asked me
if I was available to do a reading of his *important* new play.
Was how he said "important" that made me immediately say
"Yeah, sure, when?!" He said, "Tonight!" I went, "What?!"
He begged me, I could hear the desperation in his voice! So I
said, "Okay, sure, I'll be there." You'd think I'd offered him a
kidney or something. He stopped crying, made me swear that
I wouldn't *disappoint* him, that I'd be there. I'm telling you
all this . . . I knew he needed me. Perhaps it was my talent.
. . . He *knew* I was probably the only actress he could trust
with his *important* new play

You have to understand, we're artists, we support each
other; share our gifts. *(Sincerely)* So it should be obvious that
there'd no reason, *absolutely NO . . . !* Look, I have no idea
what happened. I don't know where his words went. I had
nothing to do with their disappearance from the script. I was
sitting there ready to read, but all the pages were blank! For
Gods sake, I'm not a word thief! I'm an *actress,* words are
the cushion I lay on. Without them I'd be forced to *improvise.*
—I'm sorry, I have to go, this is all very upsetting. I have to
get back to my temp job.

KATIE

Serio-comedic
early twenties to thirties
PG
All venues

Realizing that her social life is kind of a mess, Katie shares her true feelings with her best friend at a club. She's had a couple of drinks, but is definitely not drunk.

Running Time: 1 minute 30 seconds

I remember mama use to listen to this song, this old Etta James song, "I Want a Sunday Kind of Love." Was real sad. About this lonely woman looking for a love that lasted past just Saturday night. Y'know, I think I know what that song's really about now. I mean, look at us, Yvonne. We go to these clubs every Saturday night, hang out, meet guys, make out. But it's always . . . . Y'vonne, you listening to me? Hey, put your damn drink down! Eyes over here, HERE, both of 'em! You can look at him later; Jesus.

(A beat, softer) So as I was sayin', I want a Sunday kind of love. I'm tired of . . . Eyes, Yvonne, here; HERE! He'll be just as hot in ten minutes, I swear!

Look at us Yvonne. Look what we're doing with our lives. I want more than this. Want someone that will take me out on a date, a real date. And I want to meet his family and his friends; and his friends friends. And I want him to take me home to meet his momma. And go to brunch with him. And dinner dates and movies. I want a Sunday kinda love! I'm tired of . . . !

What'sa matta'? . . . You crying? *(Moving in, softly)* C'mon, stop crying; your mascara'll run. I talk too much. I'm sorry. Guess I'm a bit of a buzz kill.

S'just a stupid song ayway. I mean, who really cares?! *(Suddenly smiling, upbeat, looking around)* Hey, c'mon, where'd that guy go; one you were looking at? He was cute; and those shoulders, right?! C'mon, dry your eyes, let's walk around, see if we can find him. *(Smiling)*. Let's check out *the men folk here*. C'mon, Yvonne, stop crying, get up, let's go. C'mon.

CHARLOTTE

Serio-comedic
fifties to seventies
PG
Film, TV, Classroom. Agent

*Charlotte, a former model, recalls a story about an unusual
photo shoot she worked on in India, back in the eighties.*

Running Time: 1 minute 50 seconds

It was India, the eighties. I was shooting a commercial,
MasterCard. I was big model back then, with Ford. We were
in an old gift shop in Jaipur; taking a break from the shoot.
I was in there with the Art Director, Harry, had the hots for
me. But I played coy, enjoyed leading him on. He was so
sexy; had this magnificent mane of salt and pepper hair. Very
macho. Anyway, we were in this old dirty, dimly lit gift shop.
There were very high ceilings in the store. When I looked up,
it was extremely dark up there. Suddenly I felt something on
my sleeve. Was like a nugget or pellet. Seemed to have fallen
from the ceiling. I looked up and noticed something was *moving* up there. I started staring at the ceiling. More movement.
And it was then that I realized that it wasn't a dark ceiling
at all. I gasped, screamed, And that's when it began! All that
movement on the ceiling, the fluttering. I called to Harry.
That's when we heard these shrill, horribly sounds!

The shopkeeper came running from behind the counter,
trying to quiet me. Bats; they were bats! Hundreds and hundreds of them! Flying, coming towards us. I grabbed Harry's
arm! They flew down on us, like a black cloud! Harry let go
of me, covered his hair with his hands. And then he screamed,
yes, like a frightened little girl. Then ran out, leaving me
standing there, terrified.

(A beat, more relaxed)

Glenn Alterman

Eventually, the owner helped get me out, apologized profusely. *Brave Harry* was outside the door. He asked me if I was okay. Suddenly he seemed *so concerned*, no longer cared about his precious hair. I wanted to throttle him, I swear! But I didn't, well, you know, he was the Art Director. I had to be professional, even if he was a coward. Told him I was fine, said, "We should get back to the shoot." And we did. And I never mentioned the incident again . . . But we both knew, we knew.

❀

CEIL (FROM *THE SEALING OF CEIL*)

Serio-comedic
thirties to fifties
PG
All venues

*After some prodding from a close friend, Ceil finally con-
fesses what she really does on her afternoons.*

Running Time: 1 minute 50 seconds

I went for a walk. Just a few blocks, Times Square. Felt
I needed to get out of here. Sometimes I need to just to clear
my head, "escape."

And I was thinking . . . Oh I don't know what I was thinking. Just went, walked, looked at all the people. It's Wednes-
day, y'know, matinee day, crowds, tourists. Was lunchtime, so
I figured I'd get a bite to eat. Stopped off somewhere, some
bar on Eighth Avenue. But I realized I really wasn't hungry, so
I ordered a drink; a vodka, "Vodka tonic!" Sat there, sipped
it. Then this man came in, sat down right next to me, next
bar stool. He smiled, I nodded; he said hello. Said his name
was Hank. Very handsome, nice eyes, eyes that look right
through ya. So we sat there, me and Hank and talked about
. . . Oh I don't know what we talked about. Then out of the
blue he told me how pretty I was. I looked at him, wanted
to say, "C'mon Hank, do I look like I was born yesterday?
Thanks for the compliment but who you kiddin'?" But I just
sat there, ate it up, let him continue. Let his compliments rain
on me like a waterfall. He was looking right at me, I mean
really looking. All that attention Fran, it felt . . . Was like it
was just the two of us there, that bar. And soon he seemed, I
don't know, "desirable." And I thought, "What the hell you
thinking?! You outta your mind?! You're married to Mike!
What are you doing?!—Then I turned to him, Hank, asked

him if he wanted to come home with me. Told him I only lived a few blocks away. He smiled, said, "Sure." Just that like,— "Sure."

(accelerating)

We left, started walking, slow at first, but than faster. Neither of us said a word. We just kept walking faster, faster! Blocks flew by. Passing people, stores! Faster, rushing! Realized, I realized, I didn't know anything about him, just his name; Hank! Finally, we got to the building here. The downstairs door flew opened! We ran up the stairs, key in, I opened the door and . . . and . . . in he came.

LUCILLE

Dramatic
thirties to fifties
G
Film, TV, Classroom. Agent.

Lucille shares some advise with a new worker in her office.

Running Time: 2 minutes, 10 seconds

You could say I stopped running for office all the time. And you know what? I ended up winning. You could say that's why I'm here today. See, I stopped trying to *please everyone all the time.* Be that girl in the office *everyone liked.* That no one had a bad word to say anything about. I'd become a master of sucking up and kissing ass. I was the office Miss Congeniality.

And I have to admit it Wendy, for a while it worked. Sure, I liked being liked, who doesn't? I liked being liked a lot! I'd do anything-everyone-asked, even the bagel boy. But I'd leave here everyday with a knot in my stomach and never knew why. Be constantly worrying that maybe *someone* didn't like how I was doing my job. and I'd go home every night and drink; to relax. Wine at first. But later I moved on to vodka. Every night after work I got drunk! And then I'd begin again, same thing, next day. I ended up with an ulcer. Miss Congeniality with a big old ulcer.

Then, I don't know, one day while I was in Mr. Engles office over in book keeping, he asked me to go downstairs and get him something from the store room. I had like ten other things I had to do. I mean he wanted me to go all the way down to the basement store room! And I don't know what possessed me, but I said "No. No, go get it yourself!";—but in a *nice way of course.* Well, if you could see the look on his . . . !

And I left his office and you know what, Wendy? I felt-*great.* Was like I'd learned a brand new word; "no." And I realized that not everyone here's gonna like *me all the time.* I could say "No" once in a while. And suddenly it felt like my skin seemed to . . . fit better. That I was more *me,* whatever that means.

I guess what I'm saying is; yeah, sure, it's good to be a team player. But you've got to save some of you for yourself, honey.

(a beat)

And you don't have to come in here eight or nine times a day asking, "Is everything okay; did I do it right?!" —*(Softly, gently)* Wendy; everything's okay. You're doing a good job. Everyone likes you here. You can stop spinning your wheels, making yourself crazy. You can stop running for office. Wendy, . . . you've already won.

CANDY

Dramatic
Late teens to twenties
PG
All venues

CANDY recalls how listening to a song by Christina Aguilera helped her make a major decision.

Running Time: 1 minute 10 seconds

Was that line in that song, Christina Aguilera's song. I was listening to it, after you left. "The funny thing about hurt people is that they tend to hurt people." And it's like I got it Gary, her words, the song; us. You'd just slapped me, and left me here, and I was crying. Then hearing her words . . . A light went on. That's you, Gary. S'what you do; you hurt people, all the time. And we all let you.

And now you come back today and want *to apologize.* "You went a little crazy?" No you didn't. It's what you do; all the time. Hurt. Your friends, your family and me. —YOU-HIT-ME! And you will never put your hands on me again!

(A beat, softly) So no apology necessary. There is no "One more chance." I don't want to see you ever again. I got it, heard it in her song. You hurt people.—Well now you can get the hell out of here and go hurt someone else!

MEN'S MONOLOGUES

CHARLES

Dramatic
thirties to forties
G
All venues

*Time: 1943. Place: The United States. A large holding
area for soldiers. Charles is sitting on a bench talking to
another man.*

Running Time: 1 minute 30 seconds

That one, there, yeah. Beautiful, huh? S'my girl; my
baby. One with the big ears. Nice, huh? I've had her for, I
don't know, about four years. Belgian Sheep Dog. Beauty,
right? People always stop me on the street to tell me how
. . . Used to have a shepherd, but she got old, sick, had to
put her—to sleep. And now I'm giving them my Bella. S'her
name, yeah, Bella. Means beautiful in Italian . . . . This uh,
just seemed like the right thing to do, y'now. They need 'em
over there, the dogs, to help I hear. Heard they got nearly
15,000 of them since beginning of the war. Amazing, huh? I
wanted to go, but couldn't; got a bad ticker. But I felt I just
needed to do *something,* y'know? For the war effort! So—I
decided to give 'em my Bella. They really need good dogs
over there, and Bella's the best. She listens, minds you.
Whatever I tell her . . . *(Gets up, still looking at the dog)* . .
. I should get goin'.
(HE doesn't, stands there, looking. A beat)
They take good care of 'em over there, right? Feed 'em,
walk 'em, keep em warm. Heard it gets *real* cold. *(A beat,
pained. Softly)* I'm doin' the right thing here, right? 'Mean
we all gotta all chip in. The war, we gotta win! . . . This is
the right thing though, right? . . . Isn't it??

MILTON

Comedic
thirties to fifties
R
Film, TV and Classroom

Milton a well dressed man meats a beautiful woman in a bar.

Running Time: 2 minutes 20 seconds

I've always believed "Clothes make the man!" So for these important business meetings I always wear my best suit, best tie, with well polished shoes. I'm the guy you want to do business with. I-look-like success!

So when that hot blonde at the bar said to me, "Nice suit, nice tie; nice." I knew right off that that lady with the white wine was a kindred spirit. She appreciated a well-attired man. And I appreciated how well that tight dress *hugged* her. So I said "May I join you?" She said "Yes." And the fun began. Chit-chat, small talk, but my mind was in the gutter. Couple of drinks later, we're sharing intimate stories. She's just divorced, going to grad school, blah-blah-blah.

I tell her about this and that, not forgetting to mention how well my meeting went. Alright, okay, I *accidentally forgot* to tell her about my wife and kids. Cause all I was thinking was *I want some of that*!

Couple of drinks more and I'm ready to score, make my move. The look in her eyes, she's practically giving it away. I whisper "C'mon, let's leave." And I'm thinking, I WANT SOME OF THAT!

She leans in. I give her a tender kiss. She rubs her face softly along mine. I'm *dying*, trying to keep it down! Wondering what she's like in bed. I can picture her naked, with no clothes on, and my suit neatly folded on a chair. Then she whispers, "You know, I'm a working girl." And I smile back, "Yeah, and I'm a working guy! "—But then she clarifies. Says, "I'm here for hire; but I bet I can make you happy."

"What?!" Is she . . . ?! But she liked my suit, she said! We are simpatico! A hooker?!

"Do I *look* like I have to *pay for it*?! Think I said "PAY FOR IT?!" little too loud. People turned, looked, stared.

"I have to leave", she said, suddenly getting up from her bar stool. She gave me a dirty look and left, saying, "Yeah, thanks for the drinks!" The heightened crease in my crotch quickly deflated. The bartender handed me the tab. I sat there in a rejected stupor . . . . Then I paid him, pulled out my cell phone, dialed. Told my wife how well my meeting went. Said I'd be home soon; yeah.

CK (From *Trespassed*)

Serio-comedic
twenties to late thirties
PG
All venues

> *CK talks about how he and his sister escaped the wrath of his parents. He's had a couple of drinks, but is not drunk.*

Running Time: 1 minute 35 seconds

We all need help, sooner or later, now and then. Especially on a rainy night, like tonight, when it's dark and late, and you've been drinking, and the spirits they are a *flowin'*. But honestly, I've had it with help. My help cup runneth . . . If anything, in my life, I've been *over-helped*. And one thing you learn after a lifetime of being helped too much is that all help, all caring, comes with a cost. And that someone's help can sometimes hurt.

My sister, Lily, she always used to help me. She was a bona fide *comforter.* When we were kids, when the shit would hit the fan. When our parents would beat us, Lily was always right there for me. My parents would be coming after us, belts with buckles, hangers, whatever was handy. Couple of drinks in 'em, and it would be like, "let's get the kids!" They'd work as a team, sort of a hunting party. And we'd hide, terrified. Lily and me, while the missiles were blaring. As our drunk parents frantically searched for their little lost lambs for a little night's slaughter. As Lily and I hid under blankets or in boxes, far away from the fray. Hansel and Gretel, hiding. Lily took care of me, was my loving protector. But who knew, that years later, she'd want pay back. Well she does—but she's not going to get it. Let her take me to court I don't care. Their money was left to me; it's mine. If they wanted her to have it, any of it, my parents, they would have said so in the will. But as it just turns out, they didn't.

CARL (FROM *THE HIGH-LOW LIFE*)

Comedic
twenties to thirties
R
Theater

*A druggie talking to his girlfriend about a book that he's
going to write.*

Running Time: 1 minute 10 seconds

(Very revved up)

This book, this book I'm gonna write, will make us a
lot of money! S'gonna make me immortal! Everyone will
know my name! People will point to me on the street and say,
"He's the dude who wrote that book!" And it'll be read *long*
after I'm dead. And little kids will sneak into libraries just to
read the x-rated parts. Their teachers will warn them, "Don't
read that man's book, it's dirty-filthy!" And I will *purposely*
write *extra porno passages* just for young boys. Cause I'm
compassionate, 'cause I care. Cause I remember when I was
a kid growin' up, how hard it was to find books with dirty
passages to stimulate my hormonal imagination. Give me
rapid release so I could move on to my manhood. And soon
the boys will tell their friends. And all their friends will buy
my book. And the girls, hearing about the boys joys in reading
my book, will want to read it too! And they'll love it, because
they'll realize, that at its heart it's a simple love story.

And then their *parents* will buy my book. 'Cause parents
always want to know what their kids are wacking off to. And
soon what was once a simple underground sensation will
become a New York Times best seller! And we'll be rich,
buy the best drugs and be stoned all the time! No more cut
rate shit, only the best drugs for you! Now all I gotta do . . .
All I gotta do—is do it!

WALTER

Comedic
thirties to fifties
G
All venues

Walter talks to some friends he recently met.

Running Time: 1 minute 30 seconds

(A bit awkwardly)

I listened, I heard you and now I believe I know what you meant. What I'm saying is, I understand, well even agree with you, yeah. And that your ideas have moved me; really. I was *touched* by what you had to say the other night. Well in a way, it's why we moved out here to the woods in the first place. To escape, y'know, people, cities, all the craziness out there.

But I have to admit, when you just *showed up* in our backyard, I was, well, at the very least, *apprehensive.* I'm sure you can understand. So when my Shirley went a bit bonkers, you must realize . . . *(Smiling)* But my kids, well you saw, they loved you right away. Maybe it's cause I've always taught them *to accept,* not prejudge. That intolerance was unacceptable! Kids found you fascinating. But Shirley and me, well, yeah, it took a little longer.

But now we've worked it through, and would like to officially welcome you here to our home with open arms.

Guess what I'm *awkwardly* trying to say here is I'm happy that you've chosen *our* home. I'm pleased that we're the family you'd like to live with. And you can stay here as long as you like, really.

So—c'mon on in! Just be careful with your *tails or whatever that . . . (Half joking)* Don't want to knock over any coffee tables. Look, if you guys can't fit through the door here, you can always live in our backyard or barn or I don't know, wherever the hell you want! And, uh, I'm not exactly sure what you eat. Or even if you even eat, but, well, don't worry about it, we'll work it out. We-will-work-it-out. So, well, WELCOME!

Ted (From *The Bagel and Brunch Scene; Revised*)

Serio-comedic
thirties to forties
G
Theater

Ted tells his wife about the breaking up of a couple that they were friends with.

Running Time: 1 minute 7 seconds

Kaput! Over, fini! She threw him out. He moved in to some motel somewhere. Some cheap place by the bridge. Left last Sunday. Bagel in hand, middle of brunch. Over what, she didn't say. All I could think was, what about the kids? But I didn't ask and she didn't mention. She was in tears the whole time; was terrible. Crying on the phone like that, hysterical. I just let her go on. What could I . . . ? She called him every name in the book. As to who'll get custody? I have no idea. Probably be part time him, part time her. You know how these things work. *Divorce*, such an ugly word.

But when you think about really, it's probably for the best. I mean they were like oil and . . . So many fights all the time. Going over there for dinner was always . . . Quarrels before drinks, arguments with the appetizers.

And the main dish every night was their fights. Was almost like they wanted an audience. Witnesses to their prosecuting each other. Well, whatever it was, whatever happened, we can't pick sides, you understand ? We gotta remain absolutely neutral, impartial, like Switzerland. Let them self-destruct if they want too. But you and me, we have to agree to bud out, bud out, no matter what.

JED

Dramatic
thirties to sixties
PG
Film, TV, and Classroom.

*JED tells a stranger about an amazing life changing event
in his life.*

Running Time: 3 minutes

Hate; yeah. Everyone. Everyone I met. Was like some uncontrollable motor inside me. This constant barrage of judgments, dislikes, mistrust. Hate. And no one was beyond reproach. I found fault with everyone. The slightest flaws, imperfections. Too tall, too short, stupid, fat, whatever. Each person I'd meet was a mass of "blemishes."

Eventually, I couldn't bare to be with anyone. I lost my job, had no friends, no family, no one. Finally ended up at some fleabag hotel downtown by the water front. I lived there alone, the king of no one, on my imaginary throne, in my own self imposed, solitary confinement.

And what I learned there in that room is that eventually it all returns to roost; it all comes back. It's just a matter of time.

Was a cold night, I was tossing and turning in my bed in my roach filled room. And it arrived. Slowly at first. Little drops seeping through the ceiling. Then it came in through cracks in the wall. And then finally, it crashed through my windows, broke the glass! Soon it was everywhere! My room was filled with it! This dark, thick, gooey . . . ! Hate; it was hate and it was everywhere! I was terrified, started screaming, calling for help! And then I felt . . . Was like there was an atomic bomb exploding in my chest; right here by my heart! The pain, I can't begin to . . . ! THE PAIN! And then,—EXPLODED!

Someone must have heard my screams, called the police, an ambulance, a hospital; emergency surgery.

(A beat, softer) They said, they told me it was the size of a very large grapefruit. That it was a huge, black tumor of some kind. The doctors said they'd never seen anything like it before. It now sits quietly in a formaldehyde-filled, glass bottle in some medical lab somewhere.

(A beat, softer, more at peace)

And now, well nothing's the same. It's all changed. *Poison into medicine.* Now I see a world filled with nothing but beauty. Beauty, love and perfection. The hate is gone; it's gone. I no longer try to figure out why it all happened the way it did for me. I just accept, and appreciate. Appreciate how God-damned lucky I am! Life . . . is good.

So—that's it my friend . . . My unbelievable, but *absolutely true,* story. Crazy, I know. Way things turn out sometimes, huh. *(Smiling, friendly)* So . . . how about that drink now? It's on me. And if you'd like, if you want, you can tell me *your* story. You can tell me about all about *your* life.

RON (FROM *LIKE FAMILY*)

Dramatic
twenties to forties
G
Theater

Ron recalls a terrifying ordeal he has just been through.

Running Time: 1 minute 15 seconds

Bryn Road, yeah, we took it to the top. Top of this hill or mountain or something. I'm not sure 'cause I was lookin' out the window watchin' the snow fall, half listening to mom yak, pop tryin' to talk, the radio. I noticed the moon had gone behind a cloud and it was pitch black outside; couldn't see a thing. And I don't know, maybe there was ice on the road, but the car started to skid, slide, to the other side. *(Accelerating)* Suddenly, we were goin' down hill, fast, very fast! Sliding! Skidding! Dad kept turnin' the wheel, but nothing! There was no doubt, Dan, we were definitely going down! Then we hit a guard rail, and I heard like a loud . . . ! A crash; we crashed through! Went over, started falling, like in free fall. FALLING! And all I could think was "Oh God, no, why now, NO?!" Then CRASH! Glass! Things flying all . . . ! Was like it was happening in like slow motion, but very fast!

(Softer) And then . . . then it stopped, just stopped. Yeah, everything—stopped; was still. Was quiet, except for the horn. Damn horn wouldn't stop! This loud . . . . ! Was like-one-long . . . BEEEEEEEEEEEEEEEEEEEEEEEEEE EEEP!!

MEL (FROM *TRESPASSED*)

Dramatic
late twenties to late thirties
G
All venues

Mel talks about his difficult relationship with his sister.

Running Time: 50 seconds

I understand her; could write a book on her. She's very complicated; you'd be surprised. I know how her mind works, how she manipulates, the way she operates. And her secrets, her dirty little secrets. She keeps 'em all concealed, like in a little box. And then one day, BANG when you least expect it. BANG-BANG! Like a jack in the box, but with an iron fist! Her secrets quickly get revealed. She's tricky my sister, have to be careful.

Anyway, don't think of this so much as a warning, it's not. Well, maybe it's a "pre-warning."

I can tell you care for her; s'great. Bet you even love her, right? She's easy to fall in love with. I love her too. I mean hell, she's my big sister, we have history. Y'know, I may even love her almost as much as you. Well, almost, maybe.

SHERIDAN (FROM *THE PAIN IN THE POETRY*)

Comedic
Adult
G
Theater

Sheridan confesses how he secretly wrote a play.

Running Time: 50 seconds

> *(Meekly)*
> I wrote a play.
> *(A little louder)*
> Did you hear what I said? I wrote a play; a full length! One act with no intermission.
> *(Finally blurting it out)*
> It's been my whole life for the last two years! Every second at work when I wasn't working I was working on it! On lunch hours, in subway stations, on stairwells! Anywhere, anytime, whenever I had a moment it was just me alone with my play!
>
> I didn't tell you about it because well, it was just too private. Something I had to do alone; something I couldn't share with anyone. *(Bitterly)* Especially *you.* Then late last night, well actually early this morning, while you were asleep, I finally finished it, on the bathroom floor, by candlelight. I didn't want to talk about it until it was down on paper. But now it is, it's over. Finished. Complete. Done!

TONY (FROM THE PECKING ORDER)

Comedic
mid twenties to thirties
R
Theater

Tony asks his boss why everyone is so strange at a business convention that they're attending.

Running Time: 1 minute 10 seconds

Let me ask you something, Sollie. You've been on these company conventions before. What's wrong with everyone?! 'Mean everyone here seems so uptight. Haven't you noticed? I mean here we all get away to this paradise, escape the day-to-day, nine to five shit. A chance to meet and greet, connect, schmooze. Don't know if you've noticed, but anybody who's anyone in this company is here. It's a smorgasbord of net-working opportunities!

Alright, so this afternoon, right after we arrived, at lunch, I'm on the buffet line. And while waiting, I start making conversation with this CEO from Idaho. Forgot his name, nice guy though. And so I'm right in the middle of a sentence, talkin' 'bout God know what, when this guy, the CEO—just walks away. What'd I say?! No good-byes, nothin'. Rude, fuckin' rude.

So I turn to the guy next to me on line, some mockity-mock from the Midwest branch. Think his name's Larry. Let's say, Larry, okay? So I say, "Larry, can you fuckin' believe that guy? Fuck him." I say. "Fuck all of Idaho! Asshole!" And I start talking' to Larry. Introduce myself, shake hands, small talk. Just being friendly, dosey-doe, y'know. When Larry, yeah Larry, him too, he walks away. WHAT I SAY?! What the fuck is goin' on with these people?!

STEPHEN

Serio-comedic
mid twenties to thirties
PG
All venues

Stephen wants to leave his lover, but keeps putting it off.

Running Time: 1 minute 25 seconds

I should go home, huh baby? Your *old man* be back from the bar soon. *(Smiling)* Might not be too good to see his handyman, here at two in the morning. How would we answer that one? Guess, I could tell him I was just *(bigger smile)* screwing in some things for him. That man can be mean.—Why the hell did you marry him?!—No, don't answer that! S' none of my . . .

What are you looking at? You're usually the one does all the talking here? Okay, don't say anything, I'll just continue with my little monologue . . . *(A beat, sincerely)* I think I love you. And that is not, as we both agreed, a good thing in any way, shape or . . . I should just get the hell . . . I'm starting to feel a little over-exposed here. But you're smiling, so it can't be too bad. I like your smile. Like to make you smile. Liked when you smiled at me that first time, at the bar. And I love your body. Every inch . . . And I am now rambling. So I AM SHUTTING UP! Leaving the premises. *(Smiling)* As always, it's been my *pleasure. (Suddenly looking concerned)* What? You crying? Was it . . . ? Why are you crying?! . . . What is it, tell me, what?! Honey, why are you crying.

M<small>EL</small> (<small>FROM</small> *T<small>RESPASSED</small>)*

Dramatic
mid twenties to fifties
G
All venues

Mel tells about how he got shot and the repercussions.

Running Time: 1 minute

Yeah, I was shot. Still got me on the pain killers. Happened in the Diamond district. I was just in the wrong place at the wrong time. Was off duty, and their store security team sucked. Next thing I knew, bang-bang. Then more bang-bangs. Then I fell down. Put me out of commission for months, man. It was serious they say. A coma, life and death, touch and go. And it was totally all their fault. I'm still seeing doctors, even today, over a year later.

But, s'gonna be a nice settlement they say. Lotta money. I'll be able to retire, travel, have a somewhat nice life. But I'll tell ya, even with what I get, no matter how much it is, S'NOTHING compared to what I *lost*. A man's a man, 'cept when he's not. There's some things I just won't be able to do anymore. It sucks man! Think you get my drift.

PAUL (FROM *THE THING'S THE PLAY*)

Comedic
twenties and older
R
Theater

An anxious playwright at a playwrights group. He's speaking to the group narrator and the rest of the playwrights in the group.

Running Time: 1 minute 50 seconds

My play, well, it's sort of . . . it's a *semi-semi* sort of autobiographical play.
(HE quickly rambles on)
It's about a difficult, distanced father son, estranged relationship. The mother, she's sort of a severe alcoholic type; maybe even a crack head. I try to keep it, you know, ambiguous. Anyway, for most of the play, she sort of sits in a stupor, in a corner, like in a coma. Until, finally, like out of *nowhere,* she jumps up and hysterically starts screaming at the top of her . . . !—Well, I don't want to say what she says; you'll see.

Then, there's the incest, abuse, plenty of pedophilia, and the *absolute* necessary nudity. And then (*trying to be secretive)* maybe, maybe, a *murder* or *murders.* But I've left that a*mbiguous* too. I want the audience to make up there own minds about that. What's real, what's not.
(Directly to audience)
Actually I'd like to hear any comments you have after the reading. Tell me if you think I made the "possible" murders, too obvious. Or do you think it's just something going on inside the crazed mind of the lead. I don't want to say too much. I like my plays to speak for themselves.

I guess the bottom line, this play is really just a simple story about a boy and his dog. Our little lead, Larry, and his puppy, Pete, well Petie. *(Suddenly very sad)* His *best friend*, well actually, his *only* friend.

(Suddenly very upbeat) But you'll notice I've tried to keep the play light, humorous. I want it to be a fun-filled family play. Something I'm hoping will be done in community theaters, even church groups. A play you could bring your kids to for their first *theater experience*. You'll notice I've even included puppets for the kids, to keep things light and playful. Kids love puppets. There is, well one scene, where a maniacal "naked" puppet, goes on a . . . But that happens VERY, VERY, FAST and mostly in shadow, so the kids probably won't even . . .. Anyway, I'm talking too much. Let's just start the reading. You guys let me know what you think after.

TOM

Serio-comedic
Any age
PG
All venues

Tom talks about a weird experience he had at the gym.

Running Time: 2 minutes 10 seconds

They called it a "psychotic break." I call it just " day-dreaming between sets." *They* said that they took me out on a stretcher. Stretcher?! Yes, I did do some stretching before working out, but that was on a mat, stationary. They said it took *two* doctors to hold me down. Only two guys I remember were the two trainers, spotting me so I wouldn't drop the weights.

They also said that I was incoherent and making grunts. Sure, heavy weights can be strenuous. Sometimes you need to allow your alpha male out.

(Looking around) Have they redone this locker room? Looks different. Anyway, I should get undressed, take a shower. All of this "they said, I said" stuff is giving me a headache.

—Anyway, what I'm saying is that there's two sides to every coin, and two points of view to every *supposed* crime. Yeah, those two guys at the gym pissed me off. They were hogging the weights! So I sat there, waiting; WAITING! They saw me sitting there and didn't care. They knew I was in a rush. But lifting a couple of dumbbells over your head is not, I repeat, NOT an act of aggression, as they claimed. It was an exercise to develop my biceps. I was just doing it in rapid succession. And no, I did not *hurl* the dumbbells-at-anyone. Or at those mirrors in the gym. I have no idea how they broke. Or why that guy was bleeding so badly from his head.

(Calming himself) I was sitting in my own little world, between sets, waiting. I am now going to get undressed. I shall soon be as naked as a jaybird. Strange phrase, naked as a jaybird, don't you think? So untrue, too. The jaybird has a beautiful coat of blue and white feathers. And when's the last time you actually saw a *naked* jaybird?

(Smiling, a strange smile) There, made you smile. Just wanted you to see that I have a sense of humor. So no, I committed no crime. Didn't hurt anyone or destroy anything. And you'll soon see that when I'm totally naked, like that jaybird, I have absolutely *nothing to hide.*

THOMAS (FROM *THE THINGS THE PLAY*)

Serio-comedic
Any Age
G
TV, Film, Agents Office

Thomas talks about what he went through to write something.

Running Time: 2 minutes 45 seconds

Anything, everything. Whatever it took, whatever it takes! I'd focus, but then find myself distracted. Then return to my desk to do more rewrites, reshaping. Change a line, a word. NO, that's not right, that doesn't say it! Rip it out of the printer, start again. Play Frisbee with a phrase. Then, frustrated, look out a window, pet my cat, watch T.V., make a kettle of tea. Pretend I'm relaxed. Tell myself "Yeah everything's just fine." Pretend this isn't driving me crazy! Make believe I jut happen to be sitting here, alone, four in the morning, sipping some tea, no reason at all. Like I couldn't care less, right? But actually, I-couldn't-care-MORE!

You wonder sometimes, you know? You wonder is it really worth it? And sitting there at your desk, you wonder, why? Why am I wasting my time? Who cares? I mean really, who cares?! And soon your creative tinker toys and gardens that were about to bud, close down for what might be—a *long, deadly winter*. So I sit back down, console myself, say, "Yes, it matters." Someday, someone will see this, I say. They may even be *moved.*

I put down my hardly touched tea and return to what looks like a huge tornado forming at my desk. Ominous; scary. And soon the winds really start to blow. And I allow myself to be sucked in, taken away! And it takes me higher and higher! Soon I loose all sense of myself! I surrender.

Inward, upward! No sense of time or place! I disappear; evaporate!

(Softer) . . . And then, when it's finally over, it gently spits me out, and I land back at my desk. Quiet, calm, exhausted,—but exhilarated. I am where I was, same seat, same desk. I look down at the words on the page and—they suddenly make sense to me. There is meaning I didn't know I meant. And where I am now is where I wanted to be in the first place. The furniture's been rearranged even though it's exactly in the same place. I read what I wrote. I read what I wrote and—am *satisfied.* The storm is over. The room is quiet.

I get up, big stretch. Take the pages, leave the room, open the front door to my house, and look out. Morning. Something in me says, "Yes." Just that one word, "Yes." And that "yes" resonates through all the rooms in my house. I stand there on the front porch as the sun comes up. I stand there holding the pages. I hold the pages filled with my words, my thoughts. I hold them; hold them close.

TED

Serio-comedic
mid twenties to fifties
G
Theater

Ted tells his girlfriend about a revelation he had at the dentists that day.

Running Time: 1 minute 30 seconds

My tooth, yeah; you were right. Finally took care of it today. Yup, you were right; just like always. Like you said, "Why remain in pain?" So I saw the dentist and like you said, he said it was infected, had to be removed. So now it's out and I feel a lot whole better. No more suffering, no more pain. Made me think you know*, why do we maintain the pain*? Why do we continue? Think you might know where I'm going with this. 'Cause you're smart. College grad, as you constantly like to remind me.—

Well, stupid old me made a smart decision today. Want to hear?—I want out. I think we've both known for a long time we are so over. So why maintain the pain? We've been coasting on fumes for . . . P*retending* everything's alright. But we both damn know it's definitely not. And we're not *fixable*. We are past our expiration date. Hell, we don't even like each other anymore.

And so while I was sitting in that dentist's chair, floating on nitrous, it became so clear. It took an infected . . . God, I *love* nitrous! And y'know, now I feel really pain free. For the first time in a long time. Pain free, relieved, and, I don't know, maybe even a little—*smart.*

HAROLD (FROM *SOLACE*)

Dramatic
Adult
G
Theater

Harold recalls hearing the evening prayers from a synagogue near his apartment when he was a child.

Running Time: 1 minute 10 seconds

(Tenderly remembering, softly)

Moon light, shadows on the ceiling. I was just a kid, a young boy, almost asleep. And then it would start, every Friday night. Just as I was dozing; the davening would begin, from the synagogue across the street. The men, together, praying. The Cantor, singing; his deep, glorious voice filling my room with his warm, *comforting* tones. Then soon the rest of the congregation would join in. It was almost like they were right there in my room with me, singing good night lullabies. Their warm cries, tender voices, *flooded* my room. Their shadows seemed to surround me, circling me in my bed; *protecting me.* I was a kid, awake, but nearly asleep. It was like they'd come there to shield me, *protect me.* And now nothing, no one could get into my room. The arguments and fights; my parents, always yelling, screaming; all the time! Not now, no. I was safe in my room and it was sealed.

And soon the ceiling would disappear, and the walls would fall away and I'd leave my bed, and slowly float up into the dark, into the night. Friday. *(Softer)* And I was almost, almost asleep. It was another Friday night, and the rabbi's were there.

TOM (FROM *AFTER*)

Dramatic
Mid twenties to forties
R
All venues

*Tom reveals a clandestine meeting that he use to have every
week in a health club steam room.*

Running Time: 1 minute 30 seconds

There was a steam room at the gym where Hank and I worked
out. Wasn't very well lit and it was always filled with, well, steam.
It began one time when he spotted me, helped me with the
weights. I finished my set and said something like "Thank
you, appreciate it." He smiled, I left, went to the locker room.
Then, a little later we sort of bumped into each other in the
steam room. Accidentally brushed up against each other.
We both stood there, didn't move, didn't say anything. Just
looked at each other and . . . Then almost at the same time,
we touched. Just . . . touched each other. My hand on his
shoulder, his hand on my chest. We stood there, touching,
staring at each other, didn't say a thing. Silence, except for
the sound of the steam. Then we touched some more, face,
hips, everything. Slowly, gently. And that was it, that was all.
We left, without saying a word. But eventually it became a
regular . . . The steam room, we'd meet there, many times and
. . . I know this might sound crazy, but every time we met it
was more meaningful. The touches, more caring, sensitive.
Then kisses, caresses, embraces. Then just holding each
other. Hank was a very loving man. I know that sounds . . .
Especially since we never really said anything except "Hi"
and "Bye." But I knew it, could feel it; I *knew* him. We knew
more about each other without words, than a lot of people I
know who talk all the time.

MIKE (FROM *THE PECKING ORDER*)

Dramatic
fifties to sixties
R
All venues

Mike talks about how success nearly killed him.

Running Time: 1 minute 45 seconds

Nothing, nothing mattered Tony, nothing at all! I was fuckin' ruthless, reckless! Was my way or the highway! Did whatever the fuck I wanted. And as for work, well, I was ambition-personified! Always-got-what-I-wanted! And wherever I passed there were bodies on both sides of the road. I was a warrior, a terminator! And Tony, with success comes perks. You work hard, you're rewarded. And this company can be very generous. Nice cars, expense accounts, raises up the wazoo! Life as it should be lived. Had it all. Beautiful home, beautiful wife. You've seen my wife, a knock out, right? And we've got two picture perfect kids NOT on drugs. So you see I had it all, the whole megillah!

(a beat)

But there's a part of the picture they never discuss, never tell you. You always have to be one step ahead of everyone.

So you wake up one morning, put on your shirt, tie, Armani suit, go the office, have your coffee, kibbutz a bit with the bagel boy, turn on your lap top, and you're off and running. The pace starts picking up. And you look around, see all these young kids catching up. Thing start going faster! Orders coming in, phones, faxes, e-mails. You've got a good pace going, but you find yourself a bit out of breath. By four o'clock you're huffing and puffing. By five, you're fuckin' sweating. You realize you're not as young as you used to be.

And those kids, they're catching up, they are! So you run faster, FASTER, look, run, look run! LOOK!

(A beat, softer, slower)

Until that day, sitting at my desk. Pain, my chest. Then down my arm. Knew, I knew. I reached for the phone . . . . But then it went dark. Thought I was dead. —And, well, well, as we know now, it's never been the same since. I'm now *here,* in this small outer office.

ROBIN (FROM *SECOND TIERS*)

Comedic
fifties to sixties
R
Theater

> *Here, Robin 'from Batman and Robin', now middle aged, living in Key West with his lover 'Jimmy Olsen, (from Superman comics), tells a story about his ex, Batman.*

Running Time: 50 seconds

And how Alfred *loooved* helping Bruce, er, Batman, in and out of that Bat suit. Alfie'd be glued to the night sky waiting, no *hoping* for the Bat signal so he'd be able to dress his "Master Bruce." Bruce thought it was funny, I thought it was kina creepy. Anyway, Alfred didn't care very much for me either. Thought I wasn't "worthy enough," Y'know, the whole Wayne family pedigree. Eventually DC comics "arranged" for Bruce's marriage, just for show. They had too, there were too many rumors.

But some things never change. Last I heard, poor Bruce was secretly sneaking off to cruise men's rooms in the Gotham City Mall. I understand he's a regular tea room, toe tapper. Pretty pathetic, if you ask me. But I kind of feel bad for him, y'know. Eh, well, s'ancient history, a long time ago.

PAUL (FROM *THE THING'S THE PLAY*)

Comedic
thirties and older
R
Theater

A playwright at a playwrights group. He's speaking to the group narrator and the rest of the playwrights in the group.

Running Time: 1 minute 10 seconds

Just to keep the cast of my play, small, I have two actors playing multiple roles. You know, today most community theaters don't have much of a budget, so I've purposely constructed the scenes where our actors can exit as one character and then QUICKLY re-enter as another. Wearing a wig or a condom, or carrying a bag, or a machete, whatever.
(Indicating one of the actors)
Now Carl, Carl here, will be playing the abusive father, the totally out of it, drug counselor, the detective, the maybe (quick coy smile) or *maybe not,* child molester, the angel of death, the gay, even though *he says* he's really *straight,* piano teacher, and, *(smiling, tenderly)* oh, yeah, our little lead character, eight year old, *Larry.*

Naiomi here, will be playing his mother, the crack prostitute, the *legally* blind mother superior, the lesbian wrestler with osteoporosis, the little girl who loves to play doctor with Larry "way too much", and about a dozen other smaller roles. And, oh yeah, she'll also be doing the off-stage voice, well actually, crying whimper, of Larry's dying dog, Petie. So . . . I guess that's about all you need to know for now about the characters . . . .

(Nervously, a joke) Without *much a Jew,* here's my new play, *(Then suddenly very sincere)* "Love Song for Little Larry."

HARRY

Dramatic
thirties to fifties
PG
Theater

Homeless, a victim of a hurricane, Harry talks to a passerby.

Running Time: 1 minute 35 seconds

> *(Talking to a stranger on the street, a bitter man)*
> Don't make me beg, cause I won't. I-don't-beg. I realize how this looks, homeless guy trying to score some money for booze. But no, I'm-not-that-guy. And yeah, sure, I got drunk last night, and the night before. So what, I drink, so what!
>
> Few months ago, had we come across each other like this, I'd have snubbed you too. Like I imagine you're about to do. Suppose you're just waiting for my floor show to end, huh? —Want more? Okay, sure. History. I had a family, a house. And then y*e hurricane came!* Long Beach, where we lived, is now long gone. As are my wife and son, Sam. *They just didn't make it.* Oh, I'm sorry, have I buzzed killed your coffee? Told ya, if you don't like it, walk away. . . . Okay. —So I went from being that guy, just getting by, paying monthly mortgages to . . . here, now, *chatting* with you. I'm this guy now! And yes I will buy booze if you give me some money. I got news for you, there's a kind of freedom out here that's refreshing. I can say whatever the fuck I want! *(Directly to stranger)* When you got nothing,—you got nothing to lose.
>
> Look, I'm not out here for your entertainment pleasure. I'm on a cardboard box on a corner. And it's the end of show.
>
> *(Looking at him)* Just realize, remember, I'm you, yes,— with a twist a fate.

(A harsh whisper) I am you!

—So, money, yes or no? If not, just walk away, you are *obstructing my view*. And suddenly . . . I'm tired of talking to you.

LYLE

Dramatic
thirties to forties
PG
Film, TV, Classroom. Agent

LYLE talks about the unusual seduction he does in bars.

Running Time: 3 minutes 20 seconds

(A gentle man. He speaks softly)

I always know them. Well, I can usually spot them, right away. It's like a sixth sense or something. They're usually the ones talking too loud, making with the jokes, laughing too loud. Talking; talking to whoever's around, next to them, next bar stool. Maybe their friends, maybe not. Maybe they're people they just met, I don't know, doesn't matter. So I sit, and wait, and watch. I want to be sure.

—I like bars that are bars, not clubs or lounges. Just good old-fashioned *drink bars* where people can sit and talk and hear. And the lighting's usually dim, and the music's not too loud.

So soon I'll have a drink or two to loosen up. As I continue to watch them. I need to be certain. By now I know all the signs.

As the night goes on, they get louder and their laughter . . . It's usually around then that I mosey over, get closer, a bar stool nearby. Let them see me, know I'm there. By now they're up on their drinks and are very accepting of all new friends. And so I ingratiate myself, let them know I think they're funny; as I laugh at their unfunny jokes. As the drinks keep coming.

And soon, well sooner rather than later, the two of us become engaged in some frivolous conversation about . . . . doesn't matter. So I suggest that we move away from the bar, somewhere quieter. "Sure", they'll say. And we do. Perhaps to a darkened corner somewhere, or maybe a small out of the way table. And soon, somewhere in that shadow, I look into their eyes and ask, *(Very softly, caring)* "So, what's going on?" Perhaps it's how I say it, like I mean it, like I really want to know. Because usually at that moment, their expression changes, they look at me as if... as if for the very first time. I mean here we've been talking . . . And so I say it again, *(Softly, sincerely)* "What; what's going on? Tell me." Then there is that moment where the tide changes, where the curtain opens. Where everything is different than it was just a moment before. And then they talk, begin *really* talking; but now their voice is much softer.

   (A beat)

   Sometimes . . . sometimes it's about grief. Sometimes, it's about the end of a long love affair or a marriage that ended. Or sometimes it's about something that happened a long time ago—something that still haunts them. But it always seems to be about loss. Pain. And then they talk, and talk and talk. But they usually speak very softly. And then they cry; almost always. And sometimes I cry with them. Maybe even hold their hand. Finally . . . I feel. Finally I feel what . . .! *(A beat)* And sometimes they make these small childlike sounds. Not words, but sounds. And I sit there, and listen, and let them know I'm there. Because in that moment I care very much. We are not strangers anymore. And we both sit there until, well, there's nothing more to say, so we're silent for a while. There's just bar noise and music. And perhaps someone else laughing too loud at the bar. And I know it's time for me to go. And I do; without much fanfare. Sometimes I tell them my name, my first name. And sometimes I don't. I just leave, smile, say good night, wish them the best. And then I go home.

THOMAS

Serio-comedic
thirties and older
G
All venues

A gentle, clean shaven man. Thomas tells the story of how he grew a beard.

Running Time: 2 minutes 5 seconds

I just didn't shave for a day or two. Never had one, so I thought, why not? You get so tired of seeing the same old face day after day. So I just let it rip; stopped-shaving. And soon it started, began, it *grew*. At first I just looked unkempt, almost gave in. But something in me persevered, let it continue. And like thick moss covering a house, every day there'd be more and *more*! I felt myself transforming. Becoming more confident, bolder. My voice deepened. You have to understand, I was always the guy no one noticed. But then, as it grew, I looked like a lumberjack. Women started staring; women winked! Men became jealous, yeah! I was the cock of the roost. Hemmingway! Wolverine! My walk became a swagger. I became King Kong! And my beard kept growing!

Soon I realized, "Hey, there's no need to talk. A man with a beard doesn't have too. I began growling, grunting; eating raw meat. No need now to introduce myself to the ladies, I'd just grab them, pull them into me. Rub their faces across my manly beard. Saw looks of ecstasy in their eyes. Then I'd release them, as they'd run off, *joyfully.*

(A beat)

When the police came, I smiled, growled a bit, thumped my chest for them. I'm sure they were impressed. Because they knew, could tell, I was the king of the jungle! And that's why they brought me here. Here, where I roam among others like you. Where people gather applaud me, respect me! *(Stroking his "not there" beard)* Look how long it's grown. Took years! And now . . . now it covers me at night, my beard. It's my blanket. Keeps me warm, safe, protects me. It's my best friend. *(Stroking his imaginary beard)* Look at it. It's something, huh?! LOOK! ADMIRE; MY BEARD!

SEARS (FROM *TRESPASSED*)

Serio-comedic
thirties to fifties
G
All venues

Sears tries to persuade a lady friend to assist him in a crime.

Running Time: 40 seconds

You just have to follow the bread crumbs, baby. I know what I'm doing, trust me. They'll say it was an accident, an ACCIDENT! A fall, fall, that all. Not a shove or push, nothing done on purpose. 'Course not. And when they find him, it'll be obvious. Guy was unhappy, a messed up drunk. A FALL, that's all; shit happens.

. . . And later, when it's safe, maybe a few months, we'll meet up in Mexico. Marguerites by the pool, hired help by the handful. Postcards to our friends, saying, "Having a wonderful time, wish you were here."

I know what I'm doing baby, you gotta trust me. Follow the bread crumbs.

TOM (FROM *TRESPASSED)*

Dramatic
forties to fifties
G
All venues

Tom recalls the night a friend committed suicide.

Running Time: 55 seconds

He called me that night, Sears. You can check my cell phone, you'll see. He was drunk, out of his mind; told me he was going to off himself. I tried keeping him on the phone, y'know, to talk him out of it, but . . . . Got there as fast as I could. He's a buddy from way back, the police academy. S'been having a rough time. Three bad three marriages, and as I'm sure you heard, he didn't get that bump up to detective. That . . . that really threw him, he really wanted it. Anyway when I got to the address he gave me, the door was wide open. Looked around, called him. The wind was blowing the curtains in the windows. Kept calling him, looked everywhere. Then finally I went over to the window, out to the terrace, looked down. I hadda turn away . . . . He was a good friend, a good man; shame.

JOE

Dramatic
mid fifties to seventies
R
All venues

*Joe tells his partner about bumping into an old friend of
theirs at the barber shop.*

Running Time: 1 minute 40 seconds

Saw Kyle today. He looked . . . different. I don't know,
scary. I was in the barber shop on Seventh Avenue getting
a haircut. Saw him in the mirror, almost didn't recognize
him. He looked *strange*. I watched him for a while. He was
mumbling to himself. Then he said something to one of the
barber's. Asked him if this was the right place to get a hair
cut, *the barber shop.* He really seemed out of it. The look in
his eyes, something had happened to him.

After my haircut, I went to get my coat. Was hanging right
near where he was seated. He saw me, smiled, said, "Joe, hey
man, how you doing!?" I could smell scotch on his breath,
wasn't even noon. He stood up, said . . . " See, I'm still here!"
Can you believe it, man?! *(Very loud) I'm still-fuckin-here!"*
Everyone in the barber shop turned around, looked. Told me
he'd been in some nursing home. Had been hooked on coke
and meth, but now he was fine. All I knew was I wanted to
get out of there as quick as I could.

Maybe it was the H.I.V. or the medications they have
him on, I don't know. He was our friend, Steve, remember?
We were all so close. Even shared a house on the Fire Island.
We used to hang out, discos, dinner parties. What happened?!
I just wanted to get away from him, get out of there! I said
"Kyle, you take care of yourself, you hear me?" I took out
a twenty dollar bill, put it in his pocket. He sort of smiled,

looked confused. I left, ran around the corner, down Eighth Avenue. Kept running; running! Till I stopped by a parked car somewhere, bent down, threw up. Just stood there, Steve. I just stood there and cried.

GLENN

Dramatic
Adult
G
Theater

Glenn returns to his lovers home, hopefully to reconcile.

Running Time: 1 minute 9 seconds

Sometimes you wonder; you do. Well anyway, I did, tonight. Was at my place and thought, well, tried to figure us out, understand *us*. Tried to come to some kind of *conclusion*! But I couldn't. I could no longer just sit there anymore, not do *anything*. So I left, got in the car, drove over here. There was no wrong turn on a highway. Or panic in the middle of the night. Or some rash . . . I made a decision. I decided. And HERE THE HELL I AM!

Now don't you feel a little foolish? Aren't you maybe, I don't know, pissed or- *embarrassed?*—Honey, y*ou win. Okay? You are the winner!* The mountain's come to Methuselah, the prodigal son has returned. And soon the kissing will begin again; it will. I'm sure. And there'll be hugs and heartfelt apologies. Least that's what I'm hoping for. How I pictured it on the drive over. And we will go back to where we left off; when we were happy. (Smiling) So open your arms, baby. Don't just stand there looking so—shocked. Make like you're happy, like you missed me. Make like you really want me to be standing here! Just gotta let bygones be bygones, baby. I will not hurt you, you know that.

Hurt? . . . Hurting . . . No baby, that . . . that's your game. You're the one who hurts here.

ROBIN (FROM *SECOND TIERS*)

Comedic
fifties to sixties
R
Theater

Here, Robin 'from Batman and Robin', now middle aged, living in Key West with his lover Jimmy (Jimmy Olsen, from Superman comics), tells him about an incident that occurred one time when he was in bed with Batman.

Running Time: 50 seconds

Always amazed me how no one ever outed *Miss Alfie—Alfred*. Batman's servant, indeed. 'Mean he was so obvious, so fey. S'funny how if you carried a tray and wore a tux back then, you could get away with anything.

You know one time we caught him watching us doing it? Yeah, Bruce and me were going hot and heavy in the Bat bed, and I noticed the eyes in a painting on the wall were moving, staring. I stopped, said "Bruce, your painting, look! He jumped up, got out of bed, ran out into the hall. Saw Alfred "pretending" he was dusting something. I mean there's Bruce, buck naked. Well, I'm sure Miss Alfie got an eyeful. 'Mean they didn't call Bruce the "bat" for nothing. Anyway, Alfred sort of apologized and swished off with his duster. And Bruce came back to bed. We both had a big laugh.

KELLY

Comedic
Adult
R
Film, TV and Classroom

Kelly tells his previous lover that he now has a new lover in his life.

Running Time: 1 minute 45 seconds

(Sincerely)

I'm sorry Sally, but I've moved on. There's another woman, Wendy. And I believe she's the *one*. We have something very . . . It's hard to describe.

(Looking at her) Sally, c'mon, please, stop looking at me like that. That won't work. I told you, it's Wendy. She "listens", "hears me." Something you never . . . . Face it, the only time we ever *really* talked was when we made love. And that wasn't a conversation. Was you giving me orders. "Do this; do that!", "Higher" "Deeper."

I'm sorry, but I found it very "belittling!" I was just your boy toy. Now I have a woman . . . We have mutual *re-spect!*

(Looking at her) What are you doing? Sally, put your blouse back on. That-won't-work. I told you . . . Look, standing there with your blouse off, looking all sexy like that, will not work! I'm *immune*! I'm in love!

(A "weak" order) Please, . . . put your *skirt* back on. Look, you standing all sexy like that, in those sexy . . . I've got a girl . . .

(His tone suddenly changes) I never saw those panties before, they new? *(Weakening)* Is that Mickey and Minnie Mouse? It is! *(Half smiling)* Sally, that's *obscene! Mickey*

and Minnie are . . . ! (*Half smiling*) That's FILTHY!

(*Smiling*) No. No, leave your bra on! I don't need to see your . . . . Sally! *(A beat, staring, weakening even more)* Do you . . . ? You want a hanger for you clothes? *(A beat, realizing)* Oh, shit, Wendy will be here any . . . . Guess I don't have to answer the door, right? (*Smiling*) . . . Are you going to throw your bra at me ? *(Getting on his knees, smiling)* Bet'cha I can catch it in my mouth -like a seal; like a trained seal. Would you like that, huh? Want me to catch it ? Toss it, I'll catch it like your trained seal. That what want, huh? Tell me Sally, just . . . Tell me what you want.

SHERIDAN (FROM *THE PAIN IN THE POETRY*)

Comedic
thirties and older
PG
Theater

> *Sheridan confesses to his wife why he felt compelled to start yet another play.*

Running Time: 1 minute

> *(Filled with guilt)*

I tell you I haven't written another word! But . . . well I've been having these "thoughts." Snippets, little snippets of dialogue. This two character scene keeps playing over and over in my head. Alright, I admit it, YES, I'm thinking writing about another play!

> *(A beat)*

I was lying there on the bathroom floor last night; satisfied, content. Holding my just completed play lovingly in my arms. Caressing it, fingering the folder. Satisfied. When I heard the faucet drip. Drip, drip-drop; a lovely sound, really. I gently put the play down by my side, and just listened to the water for a while. Drip, drip-drop, drip-drop. Sounded like, I don't know, little feet. Little tiny, *tap-dancing feet.* I lay there on the floor for I don't know how long; just listening. When suddenly it hit me, this thought; maybe, maybe a musical!

DAVE (FROM *NOBODY'S FLOOD*)

Dramatic
Mid fifties to seventies
G
Theater

Dave tells his son about a strange nightly ritual that his wife does every night.

Running time: 50 seconds

She's got a new thing now, your mother. Washes floors, late at night, yeah. Started about a month ago. One night, I'm sleeping, hear something outside the door. Get up, and I see your mother on the floor. She's on her hands and knees with a bucket, washing, brushing the floor. It's like three in the morning! And she's not just brushing, Barry, she's scrubbing. Scrubbing like her life depended on it! Like she was trying to get *under* the wood. I asked her "What are you doing?" She made a mean face at me, said, "We had a flood, a bad flood!" That was it. Told me to go back to bad. I just looked at her. "Go back to bed!" she said.

Barry, there was no flood here; never. There was nothing. But every night, every single night, it's the same thing. "We had a flood. Go back to bed, GO BACK TO BED!"

Rᴏʙ (Fʀᴏᴍ *Fɪғᴛʏ, Wɪᴛʜ Mɪᴄᴋᴇʏ*)

Dramatic
fifty
G
Theater

Rob tells his partner about a terrifying incident that happened a few minutes before.

Running Time: 1minute 25 seconds

You were inside, balcony doors were closed. And I was enjoying the fireworks. Feeling good and . . . When, I don't know, I felt like a chill. Suddenly it was like I wasn't alone. Was like there was somebody or, I don't know, *something* out here with me. I looked around, nothing, no one. But I started getting nervous. Started pacing back and forth. I have no idea why, I just did. Felt like "it", whatever the hell "it" was, was following me.

I called to you, inside; screamed your name. But it was like my voice had no sound. Was like I was in a dream, screaming. I started running from one end of the balcony to the other! Finally I sat down in the chair there, pulled my head in; covered it with my hands. I was tying to hide, *but from what* I didn't know. I could feel it circling me. I was like a baby in a bubble. It was then, that moment, that I just *gave in*. I gave up, lowered my hands, opened my eyes, sat straight up in that chair and yelled as loud as I could, "Okay, COME GET ME YOU SONOFABITCH!!" *(A beat, softer)* I guess—I needed . . . needed to *accept*. And I did. On this balcony in that chair there. It came, and it found me. —*Middle age,* that's what it was. I know, it sounds crazy. *(Smiling, a relief)* But middle age came and found me on this balcony overlooking Disneyland on my fiftieth birthday. It cornered me, then covered me, like a new layer of skin.

DAVE (FROM *NOBODY'S FLOOD*)

Serio-comedic
mid fifties to seventies
G
Theater

Dave tells his son about the sudden change in his wife's personality.

Running Time: 1 minute

(Very upset, talking to his older son)

Ya see her Barry, huh? See what I been putting up with here? She's changed, your mother. S'like I've been telling you. She's gone from Dr. Jeckyll to Mrs Hyde. Hardly know her anymore. Nervous, hostile, smokes like a chimney. And ya see how she shakes all the time? Hardly ever talks to me anymore. And if she does talk, it's like I'm the janitor or something. *(Hostile)* "Empty the garbage!" "Turn off the TV!" She's said more to you today, then she's said to me in month

(Softening, upset)

Barry, the woman *hates* me. After all these years, I don't know who she is anymore. She refuses to see any doctors. And when she did go, they all said the same thing, that she's a time bomb ready to go off. That I needed to do something, soon. But you can't just drag somebody to a mental hospital. Barry, please, you gotta help me, here I'm desperate. Barry, tell me, what should I do?

NAT (FROM *UNFAMILIAR FACES*)

Dramatic
fifties to sixties
PG
Theater

*The 1980's. Nat shares his feelings with his partner after
a memorial earlier that day.*

Running Time: 1 minute 7 seconds

(Softly, upset)
There's no one left Joe. All our friends, they're gone.
(A beat)
I was walking around the village this afternoon after
Mel's memorial. And everywhere I looked . . . strangers,
unfamiliar faces. 'Mean we use to know everyone down here.
Every shop, a hello. Every bartender in every bar. Couldn't
pass a store without knowing someone inside. But it's all
changed. I kept walking, block after block, looking, but no
one. Went down to the piers. Was crowded, but no one I knew.
Not one person! Saw faces that looked sort of familiar, but
they were just "look-a-likes." And then I realized, dawned on
me, no one's left. *(becoming more upset)* They're all dead, all
our friends. It's become like a city of strangers. S'like I'm a
tourist here, visiting for the first time. Wondering, "Who are
all these people? Who lives here, huh? Who, Joe?! The kids
who come into our shop every day; haven't you noticed? All
new faces, "replacements!" Where'd everybody go? Where
are they?! WHO'S NEXT?! WHO'S LEFT?! TELL ME,
TELL ME; WHO?!

JOE (FROM *UNFAMILIAR FACES*)

Serio-comedic
Middle aged
R
Theater

Joe recalls an unusual night in a gay bar, many years earlier.

Running Time: 1 minute 10 seconds

Oh I was stoned, very; smoked a lot of dope in those days. Don't even remember what bar . . . *(Suddenly remembering)* Oh, it was the Stud, yeah! That dark, cruisey dump. Had been out with my friends, we got plowed. Ended up back at the Stud. Went directly to the back room to join in the feeding frenzy in the dark. Musta been in there, I don't know how long. Stumbled out, tucked my shirt in, I was a mess. Found a bar stool, sat, stared at the boys in the bar.

Then I saw this guy, way over on the other side of the bar. Cute, real sexy. We made eye contact, started cruising each other. Y'know, the *games.* But it started to get like "real intense", us staring at each other like that. So then I winked. And he, the guy, winked back. So I smiled, and he smiled back. Then I WAVED, and . . . and he . . . Suddenly, it hit me. I realized that this guy, one I'd been cruising so intensely-was me; yeah, ME! Was a mirror, A MIRROR! I had been cruising myself all along!

All of the monologues in this anthology were written by Glenn Alterman.

Contact the following for performance rights:

Monologues from:

The Pain In The Poetry, Coulda, Woulda, Shoulda
Contact Playscripts Inc. 450 Seventh Avenue, Suite 809, New York, NY 10123, info @playscripts.com

After
Contact Smith and Kraus (www.smithandkraus.com)

Nobody's Flood, Second Tiers, The Sealing of Ceil, Unfamiliar Faces, Fifty, With Mickey
Contact Arthur Rosen and Associates (Arthurrosen46@gmail.com)

Something Seen, Something Said, The High Low Life, The Bagel and Brunch Scene: Revised, Spilt Milk, Two Ladies Sitting In A Garden
Contact Mel Drucker Literary—(meldrucker@gmail.com)

Solace, The Thing's The Play, The Pecking Order, Trespassed and Like Family
Contact Fran Tory (toryfran@gmail.com)

Original monologues, contact:
The Glenn Alterman Studio, at Glennman10@gmail.com.

Glenn Alterman is a multi-award winning playwright, the author of twenty-six theater related books (including ten books of original monologues). He has had over 500 of his monologues published. He is also a screen writer, an actor, and a highly respected monologue/audition acting coach.

His books include: *Writing The 10-Minute Play, Two Minutes and Under (Original Monologues for Actors, (Volumes 1, 2, and 3), Street Talk (Original Character Monologues for Actors), Uptown (More Original Monologues For Actors), Glenn Alterman's Secrets To Successful Cold Readings, Sixty Seconds To Shine—101 One Minute Monologues, An Actor's Guide- Making It In New York (and a completely revised Second Edition), The Perfect Audition Monologue, Creating Your Own Monologue (and a completely revised Second Edition), Promoting Your Acting Career, (and the Second Edition, A Step-By-Step Guide To Opening The Right Doors), The Job Book: One Hundred Acting Jobs for Actors, The Job Book 2: One Hundred Day Jobs for Actors, What to Give Your Agent for Christmas,* and *Two Minute Monologs.*

Two Minutes and Under, Street Talk, Uptown, Creating Your Own Monologue, and An Actors Guide-Making It In New York were all "Featured Selections" in the Doubleday Book Club (Fireside Theater and Stage and Screen Division").

Several colleges are planning on including *Writing The 10-Minute Play (A Book For Playwrights, and Actors Who Want To Write Plays),* as part of their upcoming theater arts curriculum.

As a playwright, Mr. Alterman is the recipient of the first Julio T. Nunez Artist's Grant, The Arts and Letters Award in Drama, and winner of scores of playwriting awards, including being a four time finalist at The Actor's Theater of Louisville Ten-Minute Play Competition.

His play *The Pain in the Poetry* was published in 2009 *The Best Ten-Minute Plays For 2 or More Actors (*Smith and

Kraus, and published by Playscripts). His play *After* was published in *The Best Ten-Minute Plays of 2011*(Smith and Kraus). And his latest ten-minute play, *Second Tiers,* is in *The Best 10-Minute Plays of 2012* (Smith and Kraus). Many of his other plays are published by Playscripts.

Mr. Alterman's plays, *Like Family* and *The Pecking Order,* were optioned by Red Eye Films (with Alterman writing the screenplay). His play, *Solace*, was produced off-Broadway by the Circle East Theater Company (formerly Circle Rep Theater Company). *Nobody's Flood* won the Bloomington National Playwriting Competition, as well as being a finalist in the Key West Playwriting Competition. *Coulda-Woulda-Shoulda* won the Three Genres Playwriting Competition two years in a row. The prize included publication of the play in all future editions of the Prentice Hall textbook, *The Three* Genres, *The Writing of Literary Prose, Poems, and Plays,* used in college theater departments all over the country.

Mr. Alterman wrote the book for *Heartstrings: The National Tour* (commissioned by DIFFA, the Design Industries Foundation for Aids), a thirty-five city tour that starred Michelle Pfeiffer, Ron Silver, Susan Sarandon, Marlo Thomas, and Sandy Duncan.

Other plays include *Kiss Me When It's Over* (commissioned by E. Weissman Productions), starring and directed by André De Shields, *Tourists of the Mindfield* (finalist in the L. Arnold Weissberger Playwriting Competition at New Dramatists); and *Street Talk/Uptown* (based on his monologue books), produced at the West Coast Ensemble.

Spilt Milk received its premiere at the Beverly Hills Rep/Theater 40 in Los Angeles and has several dozen production in the U.S. and Europe. The *Danger of Strangers* won Honorable Mention in the Deep South Writers Conference Competition, was a finalist in the George R. Kernodle Contest, was selected to be in the Pittsburgh New Works Festival and has had over 35 productions, including at Circle Rep Lab and the West Bank Downstairs Theater Bar (starring James Gandolfini) The play was recently optioned for TV. There have been many productions of his original monologues play, *God In Bed*, both in the United States and in Europe.

Mr. Alterman's work has been performed at Primary Stages, Ensemble Studio Theater (EST), Circle in the Square Downtown, HERE, LaMaMa, in the Turnip Festival, at the Duplex, Playwrights Horizons, at several theaters on Theater Row in New York, as well as at many theaters around the country.

Mr. Alterman has been a guest artist and given master classes and seminars on "Monologues" and "The Business of Acting" at such diverse places as the Governor's School for the Arts in Norfolk, Virginia, the Edward Albee Theater Conference (Valdez, Alaska), Southampton College, Western Connecticut State College, Broadway Artists Alliance, The American Federation of Television and Radio Artists (AFTRA), the Dramatists Guild, the Learning Annex, the Screen Actors Guild, the Seminar Center, in the Boston Public School System, and at many acting schools and colleges all over the country.

In 1993, Mr. Alterman created the Glenn Alterman Studios, where actors receive monologue/audition coaching, as well as career preparation. He was named "Best Monologue/Audition Coach in the Tri-State Area" by Theater Resources Magazine and "Best Monologue Coach In New York", by the readers of *Back Stage*.

He presently lives in New York City, where he's working on several new plays, and freelances with several film companies assisting in the acquiring of plays to be made into films.

On the Web, he can be reached at:
www.glennalterman.com